I0013169

Parallel Python Programming™:

"Harnessing Concurrency and Multicore Processing for High-Performance Computing"

Ethan B. Carter

All rights reserved. No part of this publication may be reproduced, distributed, or transmitted in any form or by any means, including photocopying, recording, or other electronic or mechanical methods, without the prior written permission of the publisher, except in the case of brief quotations embodied in critical reviews and certain other noncommercial uses permitted by copyright law.

Copyright © Ethan B.Cater
(2024)

TABLE OF CONTENT

Chapter 12: Case Studies and Applications

12.1. Parallel Image Processing

12.2. Real-time Data Processing Systems

12.3. Machine Learning and AI with Parallelism

Chapter 1

Introduction to Parallel Programming

Parallel programming is a technique used to solve computational problems more efficiently by executing multiple operations simultaneously, leveraging the power of modern multi-core processors or distributed computing systems. Unlike sequential programming, where tasks are performed one after another, parallel programming divides a problem into smaller subproblems that can be solved concurrently.

The main goal of parallel programming is to enhance performance, particularly for tasks that require substantial computation, such as scientific simulations, data processing, machine learning, and rendering. By splitting work across multiple processors or cores, it is possible to significantly reduce the time required to complete a task.

Parallelism can be achieved in various forms, including:

Task parallelism: Different tasks or operations are performed simultaneously, often independent of one another.

Data parallelism: The same operation is applied to different chunks of data in parallel.

Pipeline parallelism: Tasks are arranged in stages, where the output of one stage becomes the input for the next, and each stage runs in parallel.

While parallel programming offers performance benefits, it also introduces challenges, such as managing synchronization between threads or processes, ensuring load balancing, and handling concurrency issues like race conditions and deadlocks. Modern languages, like Python, provide frameworks and libraries that abstract much of the complexity, allowing developers to focus on solving problems while efficiently utilizing available computing resources.

1.1. What is Parallel Programming?

Parallel Programming is a type of computing in which multiple tasks or computations are executed simultaneously, rather than sequentially. The primary objective is to improve the performance and efficiency of programs by taking advantage of multiple processing units (cores, CPUs, or distributed machines) that can work concurrently.

In a parallel program, large problems are divided into smaller, independent tasks, which can be processed simultaneously. This approach is particularly useful for applications that require significant computational power, such as scientific simulations, image processing, machine learning, and big data analysis.

Parallel programming can be implemented at various levels:

Bit-level parallelism: Exploits the ability of processors to operate on multiple bits simultaneously.

Instruction-level parallelism: Enables the concurrent execution of different instructions within a CPU.

Data parallelism: Applies the same operation to multiple data elements in parallel.

Task parallelism: Distributes different tasks to different processors or cores.

Parallel programming typically involves using multiple processors or cores to execute parts of the program concurrently, which reduces execution time and improves the overall performance of the application.

However, it also introduces challenges, such as managing concurrency, synchronizing shared resources, and ensuring proper task coordination. Tools and libraries in programming languages like Python (e.g., multiprocessing, threading, and asyncio) help developers leverage parallelism in their applications.

1.2. Benefits of Parallel Computing

Parallel computing offers several significant advantages, especially when dealing with large-scale, computationally intensive tasks. By distributing workloads across multiple processors or cores, parallel computing can greatly improve performance and efficiency. Here are some key benefits:

Increased Performance: Parallel computing allows tasks to be divided into smaller sub-tasks, which can be executed simultaneously across multiple processors or cores. This results in faster execution times compared to traditional sequential computing, especially for computationally heavy problems.

Faster Problem Solving: Problems that would otherwise take days, weeks, or even longer to solve using a single processor can be completed much more quickly in a parallel computing environment. For example, tasks like simulating complex systems, data analysis, or processing large datasets can be accelerated.

Efficient Utilization of Multicore Processors: Modern computers and servers come with multiple processor cores. Parallel computing leverages the power of these multicore systems, ensuring that each core is utilized optimally, thus maximizing the overall processing capacity of the hardware.

Scalability: Parallel computing systems can scale to handle increasingly large datasets or more complex computations. As workloads grow, more processing units (cores or machines) can be added to the system, maintaining or even improving performance without significant redesign.

Cost Reduction: Parallel computing can reduce the time required to complete complex tasks, which in turn reduces computational costs. For industries like scientific research or simulations, this can lead to significant savings in both time and resources.

Additionally, with the rise of cloud computing, users can rent parallel computing resources, minimizing infrastructure costs.

Handling Large Datasets: With the increasing amount of data being generated, parallel computing provides an effective way to process and analyze large datasets. Whether it's big data analytics, machine learning, or simulations, parallelism enables faster data processing and improved performance in managing these large volumes of information.

Energy Efficiency: By reducing the time required to perform computations, parallel computing can also contribute to energy savings. Shorter execution times mean less energy consumption overall, which is particularly important in large-scale data centers and cloud environments.

Improved Reliability and Fault Tolerance: In some parallel computing systems, workloads can be distributed across multiple machines, ensuring that if one machine fails, others can take over the task. This redundancy enhances the overall reliability of the system, especially in high-performance computing (HPC) environments.

Enabling Advanced Applications: Parallel computing unlocks the ability to perform computations that were previously impossible or impractical with single-threaded processing. This includes applications in fields like artificial intelligence, weather forecasting, molecular modeling, financial analysis, and more.

Optimized Resource Management: By distributing workloads efficiently, parallel computing systems optimize resource utilization. This ensures that both computational resources (like CPU and memory) and input/output operations are maximally utilized, leading to faster and more efficient task execution.

In summary, parallel computing enhances performance, scalability, and efficiency, making it essential for addressing the growing complexity of modern computational tasks and large-scale data processing needs.

1.3. The Evolution of Python for Parallelism

Python, known for its simplicity and versatility, has gradually evolved to support parallel programming, allowing developers to leverage multiple processors or cores for faster and more efficient execution of computational tasks. Over the years, Python's support for parallelism has grown, with various libraries and frameworks introduced to address the challenges of concurrency and parallel processing. Below is an overview of the key developments in Python's evolution for parallelism:

1. Early Days: Limited Support for Parallelism

In the early versions of Python, there was limited support for parallel programming, primarily because the language was designed to be simple and readable, with a focus on sequential processing. The Global Interpreter

Lock (GIL), a mechanism in Python's CPython implementation, posed a significant challenge for multi-threading. The GIL allows only one thread to execute Python bytecodes at a time, limiting the ability to fully utilize multi-core processors for CPU-bound tasks.

As a result, Python's built-in threading module was mainly useful for I/O-bound tasks (like file operations or network requests) but was ineffective for CPU-bound tasks due to the GIL.

2. Introduction of the multiprocessing Module

In response to the limitations posed by the GIL, Python introduced the multiprocessing module in Python 2.6 (released in 2008). The multiprocessing module allows developers to bypass the GIL by using separate processes, each with its own Python interpreter and memory space. This enables true parallel execution on multi-core systems for CPU-bound tasks.

The multiprocessing module supports creating and managing processes, inter-process communication, and synchronization. It is an essential tool for developers looking to take full advantage of multi-core processors in Python.

3. Development of Asynchronous Programming: asyncio

As the need for more efficient concurrency models grew, especially for I/O-bound tasks, Python introduced asyncio in Python 3.4 (released in 2014). The asyncio module allows for asynchronous programming using coroutines and event loops, enabling non-blocking I/O operations. While it is not parallelism in the traditional sense, asyncio provides an efficient way to handle thousands of tasks concurrently within a single thread.

This approach is particularly beneficial for network or disk I/O operations, where Python can handle many tasks simultaneously without the overhead of creating new threads or processes. However, for CPU-bound tasks, asyncio does not offer parallelism since it still runs in a single thread.

4. Parallelism through concurrent.futures

In Python 3.2 (released in 2011), the concurrent.futures module was introduced to simplify parallel programming. The module provides high-level abstractions for managing concurrent execution using threads or processes. Specifically, it includes the ThreadPoolExecutor and ProcessPoolExecutor classes, which allow developers to execute tasks concurrently without directly managing threads or processes.

concurrent.futures offers an easy-to-use interface for parallelism, making it easier for developers to write parallel code. It abstracts away the complexities of managing threads or processes and provides features like task scheduling and result collection, which simplifies concurrent programming.

5. Third-Party Libraries and Frameworks

As Python's standard library evolved to support parallelism, the ecosystem also saw the rise of several powerful third-party libraries designed to handle parallelism more efficiently or to address specific parallel computing needs:

Dask: A parallel computing framework for big data analytics. Dask enables parallel and distributed computing in Python and integrates well with libraries like NumPy, pandas, and scikit-learn.

Celery: A distributed task queue used to manage asynchronous jobs and workloads in distributed systems. It is commonly used for handling background tasks in web applications.

Joblib: A library designed for parallelizing simple Python functions. It's often used in machine learning and scientific computing to speed up CPU-bound tasks by utilizing multiple cores.

PyTorch and TensorFlow: Although primarily focused on machine learning, these libraries use parallelism and GPU acceleration to speed up training and inference tasks.

6. GPU Support and Parallel Computing Libraries

As Python's popularity in scientific computing and machine learning grew, the need for more powerful parallel computing capabilities emerged. To address this, libraries like CuPy, TensorFlow, and PyTorch were developed to enable GPU parallelism. These libraries use Python's interface to interact with CUDA (NVIDIA's parallel computing architecture), allowing developers to harness the massive parallelism offered by GPUs for computation-heavy tasks like deep learning and numerical simulations.

7. Python and Distributed Computing

As the scale of parallel computing continues to grow, Python has evolved to support distributed computing across multiple machines. Libraries like Dask, Pyro4, and Ray facilitate the development of distributed systems where tasks are spread across many nodes, enabling the processing of vast datasets or performing complex computations that cannot fit into a single machine's memory.

Ray: An emerging framework for distributed computing that simplifies the development of parallel and distributed applications, particularly in machine learning and AI.

8. The Future of Parallelism in Python

The future of parallelism in Python looks promising, with ongoing work to improve performance and simplify parallel programming. Some areas of focus include:

Enhancements to the asyncio module for better concurrency models.
Potential improvements to the GIL or new implementations of Python that allow better multi-threaded performance.
Increasing integration of parallelism and distributed computing for scalable applications.
More support for GPU computing, making Python a competitive language for high-performance computing.

Conclusion

Python's evolution for parallelism has come a long way, from its initial limitations due to the GIL to its current status as a powerful tool for both concurrent and parallel programming. With libraries like multiprocessing, asyncio, concurrent.futures, and the rise of GPU and distributed computing frameworks, Python has become an increasingly important language for high-performance computing. As parallel and distributed systems continue to grow in importance, Python will likely continue to innovate and evolve to meet the demands of developers working with large-scale computational problems.

1.4. Key Concepts: Concurrency vs Parallelism

While the terms concurrency and parallelism are often used interchangeably, they represent different concepts in computing. Understanding the distinction between them is important for developers when designing systems that aim to improve performance or manage complex workflows. Below is an explanation of both terms and how they differ.

1. Concurrency

Concurrency refers to the ability of a system to manage multiple tasks or processes at the same time, but not necessarily simultaneously. In a concurrent system, tasks may start, run, and complete in overlapping periods, but not necessarily at the same exact moment. The key feature of concurrency is that it allows for the management of multiple tasks in a way that makes progress on all of them, even if they are not all executing at the same instant.

Key Characteristics of Concurrency:

Interleaving Execution: Concurrency is often implemented by interleaving the execution of multiple tasks. This can be achieved by switching between tasks rapidly so that it appears as if tasks are being executed simultaneously.

Single or Multi-Core: Concurrency does not require multiple cores or processors. It can be implemented in single-core systems where the operating system or the programming model switches between tasks.

Efficiency in I/O-bound Tasks:

Concurrency is especially beneficial for I/O-bound tasks, like reading from a disk, network communication, or handling multiple user requests, where tasks spend a lot of time waiting for input or output operations.

Examples of Concurrency:

A web server handling multiple HTTP requests by processing one request, then switching to another, and so on, in a non-blocking manner.

A single-threaded application that uses callbacks or event loops to handle multiple tasks (e.g., using Python's asyncio module).

2. Parallelism

Parallelism, on the other hand, is the execution of multiple tasks or processes at the exact same time, typically by using multiple cores or processors. The goal of parallelism is to speed up a computation by performing many operations concurrently. It involves dividing a task into smaller sub-tasks, each of which is executed simultaneously, either on different cores or processors.

Key Characteristics of Parallelism:

Simultaneous Execution: Tasks are executed at the same time on different processors, cores, or machines, which results in a reduction in total execution time.

Multiple Processors/Cores: Parallelism requires multiple processing units (either cores within a single CPU or multiple CPUs) to run tasks simultaneously.

Efficiency in CPU-bound Tasks: Parallelism is especially useful for CPU-bound tasks, where computations require substantial processing power, such as scientific simulations, data analysis, or image processing.

Examples of Parallelism:

A multi-core processor running multiple threads of a program at the same time, where each thread performs a part of the computation.

A large data processing task, such as sorting or matrix multiplication, split into multiple tasks and computed in parallel on different processors.

Key Differences Between Concurrency and Parallelism

Aspect	Concurrency	Parallelism
Definition	Managing multiple tasks at once, but not necessarily at the same time	Performing multiple tasks simultaneously.
Execution	Tasks are interleaved, taking turns to execute on a single processor.	Tasks run at the same time on multiple processors or cores.
Goal	Improving the system's ability to handle multiple tasks.	Speeding up computation by executing tasks simultaneously.
Required Resources	Single-core or multi-core (can be implemented	Requires multiple processors or

	on a single processor).	cores.
Focus	I/O-bound tasks, where tasks spend time waiting.	CPU-bound tasks, where computation is the bottleneck.
Approach	Tasks are divided into smaller pieces and handled in an overlapping manner.	Tasks are divided into smaller pieces and executed at the same time.
Example	A web server handling multiple client requests at once	A parallel algorithm splitting large data for simultaneous computation.

Concurrency vs Parallelism: How They Work Together

Concurrency and parallelism are not mutually exclusive; they can be used together in the same application. A concurrent system can be designed to handle multiple tasks at once, and some of those tasks might be parallelized for even greater performance.

For instance, a web server might use concurrency to handle many incoming client requests, and for each request, the server could parallelize the work by dividing the task into smaller sub-tasks that can be processed simultaneously across multiple cores.

Conclusion

In summary:

Concurrency is about managing multiple tasks at once, making progress on each one over time, but not necessarily executing them simultaneously.

Parallelism is about dividing a task into smaller parts and executing those parts at the same time across multiple processors or cores.

Both concepts are crucial for developing high-performance systems. Concurrency is useful for handling many tasks efficiently, while parallelism provides a way to speed up specific tasks by executing them simultaneously. The choice between concurrency and parallelism (or a combination of both) depends on the nature of the problem being solved.

1.5. Challenges in Parallel Programming

While parallel programming offers significant performance improvements and efficiency, especially for computationally intensive tasks, it also introduces a range of challenges that can make development more complex. Managing concurrency, ensuring correctness, and optimizing resource usage are some of the difficulties developers face when writing parallel applications. Below are some of the key challenges in parallel programming:

1. Concurrency Issues

Concurrency in parallel programming requires careful management of how tasks are scheduled and executed to avoid issues such as:

Race Conditions: A race condition occurs when two or more threads or processes attempt to modify shared data simultaneously, leading to unpredictable results. Managing access to shared resources is critical to avoid these conditions.

Deadlocks: A deadlock occurs when two or more threads or processes are stuck waiting for each other to release resources, causing the program to halt. Detecting and avoiding deadlocks can be tricky, especially in complex applications.

Starvation: Starvation happens when a thread or process is perpetually denied access to the resources it needs because other threads or processes keep taking precedence. This can lead to some tasks never being executed.

2. Synchronization Issues

When multiple threads or processes access shared data, synchronization is required to ensure that the data remains consistent.

Common challenges include:

Locking Mechanisms: Using locks (e.g., mutexes or semaphores) to synchronize access to shared resources can prevent race conditions, but improper use can lead to performance bottlenecks. Too many locks or poorly designed locking mechanisms can slow down the program.

Deadlocks from Locks: Incorrectly acquiring locks in an inconsistent order can result in deadlocks. Managing lock acquisition carefully is crucial to avoid blocking the system.

Atomic Operations: Ensuring that a sequence of operations on shared data is executed atomically (without interruption) is often necessary for correctness. Without atomicity, other threads or processes may interfere and lead to incorrect outcomes.

3. Scalability Issues

Scaling parallel applications to efficiently utilize more processors or cores is a common challenge:

Amdahl's Law: Amdahl's Law suggests that the speedup of a parallel program is limited by the fraction of the program that can be parallelized. The more time a program spends on sequential tasks, the less effective parallelization becomes.

Load Balancing: Ensuring that the workload is evenly distributed across processors or cores is crucial for performance. If some processors are overloaded while others remain idle, the overall efficiency of the program is reduced.

Overhead: The overhead of managing parallelism (e.g., creating threads, synchronizing data, etc.) can negate the benefits of parallel execution, particularly if the tasks being parallelized are too small or simple.

4. Debugging Parallel Programs

Debugging parallel programs is more challenging than debugging sequential programs due to:

Non-Deterministic Behavior: The execution order of threads or processes in parallel programs can vary from run to run, making it difficult to reproduce bugs and find their causes. This can result in timing-related bugs that only occur under specific conditions.

Difficult-to-Trace Errors: Errors such as race conditions or deadlocks are often non-deterministic and can be difficult to detect. These errors might only appear intermittently, making them challenging to diagnose and fix.

Complexity in Reproduction: In parallel applications, reproducing the exact order of events that led to an error can be nearly impossible. This makes testing and debugging more difficult than in single-threaded applications.

5. Memory Consistency and Management

Parallel programs often share data between threads or processes, leading to memory consistency issues. Managing memory efficiently and ensuring that data is correctly synchronized across different threads or processes are crucial to avoid inconsistencies.

Cache Coherence: In multi-core systems, each core may have its own cache, leading to discrepancies between copies of data. Ensuring that all cores have a consistent view of memory is essential for correctness.

Memory Leaks: Improper management of memory in parallel programs can lead to memory leaks, where memory is allocated but never freed, leading to inefficient memory usage and eventual program failure.

False Sharing: False sharing occurs when multiple threads on different processors modify variables that are stored in the same cache line, causing unnecessary cache invalidations and reducing performance.

6. Load Imbalance

In many parallel applications, the workload is divided into chunks that are processed by different threads or processes. If the work is not evenly distributed, some threads or processes may finish early while others are still working, leading to idle processors and inefficient use of resources.

Dynamic Scheduling: In cases where the size of the tasks varies, using static scheduling (where work is predefined) might lead to load imbalances. Dynamic scheduling techniques can be used to redistribute tasks during execution, ensuring better load balance.

7. Communication Overhead

When tasks in parallel programs need to exchange data, the communication between them can become a bottleneck. This is especially true in distributed systems or multi-node environments, where data must travel over a network.

High Latency: Communication between processes running on different machines can introduce high latency, reducing the effectiveness of parallelism. Reducing communication overhead by minimizing data transfer and synchronizing fewer times can improve performance.

Bandwidth Constraints: In distributed systems, limited network bandwidth can also become a bottleneck, affecting the scalability of parallel applications.

8. Limited Tooling and Libraries

Although Python has several powerful libraries for parallel programming (e.g., multiprocessing, concurrent.futures, asyncio), there are still limitations in terms of scalability and support for advanced parallel computing techniques, such as GPU programming or distributed computing.

Fragmented Ecosystem: The diverse range of tools available for parallel programming can be overwhelming, and integrating them into a single application might require significant effort.

Lack of Standardization: Different parallel computing paradigms (e.g., multi-threading, multi-processing, distributed computing, GPU acceleration) often require different programming models, making it challenging to develop a unified approach.

9. Power Consumption

Parallel computing, especially when scaling to large systems, can increase power consumption. This is a concern for both energy efficiency and hardware longevity. Efficient parallel programming needs to balance performance improvements with power usage, particularly in mobile or embedded systems.

Conclusion

While parallel programming has the potential to significantly improve performance, it comes with a host of challenges that developers must carefully address. Issues such as concurrency, synchronization, scalability, debugging, and memory management require a deep understanding of parallel systems and sophisticated techniques. Overcoming these challenges often involves careful design, testing, and profiling to ensure that parallelism leads to tangible performance gains without introducing new problems. As parallel programming tools and techniques continue to evolve, these challenges will become easier to manage, but they will remain a core consideration for developers working in high-performance computing environments.

Chapter 2

Understanding Python's Global Interpreter Lock (GIL)

The Global Interpreter Lock (GIL) is a mechanism used in the CPython implementation of Python to ensure that only one thread executes Python bytecode at a time. This lock is necessary because CPython's memory management (specifically reference counting) is not thread-safe. The GIL prevents race conditions in the interpreter and simplifies memory management, but it also introduces some limitations, particularly in multi-threaded, CPU-bound applications.

Key Points:

Thread Safety: The GIL ensures that only one thread can execute Python bytecode at any given time, making it easier to manage Python's memory and garbage collection without the risk of corruption from multiple threads.

Performance Limitation: In a multi-core system, the GIL can become a bottleneck, preventing Python from fully utilizing multiple cores for CPU-bound tasks. While one thread runs, others must wait, which limits parallelism in multi-threaded programs.

I/O-bound Tasks: For tasks that spend time waiting (like I/O operations), Python's threading model can still be effective. Threads can release the GIL while waiting for I/O, allowing other threads to execute in the meantime.

Multiprocessing as a Solution: To bypass the GIL and fully utilize multiple cores, Python developers often use the multiprocessing module. This module creates separate processes (each with its own Python interpreter and memory space), allowing for true parallel execution.

Alternative Python Implementations: Other Python implementations, like Jython (Python on the JVM) or IronPython (Python on the .NET framework), do not use the GIL and can achieve better multi-threading performance on multi-core systems. However, CPython remains the most widely used Python implementation.

Conclusion:

While the GIL simplifies memory management and ensures thread safety in CPython, it also limits multi-threading performance, particularly for CPU-bound tasks. Developers often work around this limitation using multiprocessing or focusing on I/O-bound tasks for multi-threading.

2.1. What is the Global Interpreter Lock?

The Global Interpreter Lock (GIL) is a mechanism used in the CPython implementation of Python to ensure that only one thread executes Python bytecode at a time. This lock is necessary because CPython's memory management, specifically its reference counting system for garbage collection, is not thread-safe. The GIL prevents multiple threads from simultaneously modifying memory or objects in an unsafe way.

Key Features of the GIL:

Thread Safety: The primary purpose of the GIL is to protect internal data structures, such as the Python memory heap, from being corrupted by concurrent thread access. It allows only one thread to execute Python code at a time, making it simpler to implement memory management in CPython without complex thread synchronization mechanisms.

Limiting Concurrency: While Python supports multi-threading, the GIL limits the true parallel execution of threads in a multi-core CPU environment. Even if there are multiple cores available, only one thread can execute Python bytecode at a time, which means multi-threading does not provide a significant performance improvement for CPU-bound tasks in CPython.

Impact on CPU-bound Tasks: For programs that perform CPU-intensive calculations, the GIL is a bottleneck. Even with multiple threads, only one thread can execute at a time, limiting the potential for parallel processing and preventing Python from fully utilizing multiple CPU cores.

Impact on I/O-bound Tasks: The GIL does not prevent concurrency in I/O-bound tasks, such as reading/writing files or waiting for network responses. In these cases, threads can release the GIL while performing I/O operations, allowing other threads to run and making Python effective for tasks that are waiting on external systems.

Workarounds and Alternatives:

Multiprocessing: To overcome the limitations of the GIL for CPU-bound tasks, Python developers often use the multiprocessing module, which spawns separate processes (each with its own Python interpreter and memory space), allowing for true parallelism across multiple CPU cores.

Alternative Implementations: Other Python implementations, like Jython (Python on the JVM) and IronPython (Python on the .NET framework), do not have a GIL and can better utilize multi-core systems for concurrent execution.

Conclusion:

The GIL is a core feature of CPython that simplifies memory management but also limits the performance of multi-threaded programs, particularly for CPU-bound tasks. For many I/O-bound applications, it is not a significant issue, but for computationally heavy tasks, developers often resort to multi-processing or other Python implementations to fully leverage multi-core systems.

2.2. GIL and Multi-threading in Python

The Global Interpreter Lock (GIL) is a critical aspect of CPython, the standard implementation of Python, that directly impacts how multi-threading works in Python. Understanding the relationship between the GIL and multi-threading is crucial for developers who want to optimize Python programs for concurrent execution, especially when dealing with multi-core processors.

What is the GIL?

The Global Interpreter Lock (GIL) is a mutex (mutual exclusion) that prevents multiple native threads from executing Python bytecodes simultaneously in CPython.

While Python supports multi-threading through the threading module, the GIL ensures that only one thread can execute Python code at a time, even if the program is running on a multi-core system.

How the GIL Affects Multi-threading

Single-Threaded Execution:

The GIL essentially makes Python programs single-threaded when executing Python bytecode, even in a multi-threaded environment. If there are multiple threads, only one thread can be executing Python bytecode at any given time, and other threads must wait their turn.
This results in limited parallelism for CPU-bound tasks, as threads are not able to run concurrently on different cores.

Thread Switching:

The GIL works by switching between threads in a way that allows the system to manage thread execution.

When one thread is running, the other threads are blocked. The GIL does allow Python to periodically switch between threads, but it does not achieve true parallelism.

Python's interpreter releases the GIL when performing I/O operations, such as file reading or network communication. As a result, multi-threading in Python can still be beneficial for I/O-bound tasks where threads spend a lot of time waiting for external events (e.g., waiting for data from a server).

CPU-bound Tasks:

For CPU-bound tasks, which involve heavy computation (e.g., mathematical operations, data processing), the GIL becomes a performance bottleneck.
Even if the program has multiple threads, only one thread can use the CPU at any given time. As a result, the program cannot fully take advantage of multiple CPU cores, leading to suboptimal performance for multi-core systems.

The Impact of the GIL on Multi-threading

Limited Parallelism: Since the GIL prevents more than one thread from executing Python bytecode at once, Python threads cannot execute in parallel on multi-core systems for CPU-bound tasks. This limits Python's ability to perform multi-core parallel processing efficiently.

Threaded I/O-bound Tasks: For tasks that are I/O-bound, such as waiting for a network response or reading from disk, the GIL is less of an issue. While one thread is blocked waiting for I/O, another thread can take over and continue execution. This allows Python to handle multiple I/O operations concurrently using threads, making Python's multi-threading model useful for I/O-bound applications.

Workarounds for Overcoming the GIL
Multiprocessing:

One of the most common ways to bypass the limitations of the GIL for CPU-bound tasks is the multiprocessing module. Unlike threads, which share the same memory space, processes in Python run in their own memory space and have their own Python interpreter. Each process can run on a separate core, allowing for true parallelism and better utilization of multi-core systems. The multiprocessing module allows you to split a task into multiple processes, enabling parallel computation across CPU cores without being blocked by the GIL.

External Libraries and C Extensions:

Some Python libraries, like NumPy, leverage C extensions to perform heavy computation outside the constraints of the GIL. These libraries use C code for performance-critical sections, which can bypass the GIL and run in parallel.

Libraries like Cython or PyPy (another Python implementation) can also help bypass the GIL in specific scenarios, though these require more advanced techniques or alternative environments.

Alternative Python Implementations:

Some Python implementations do not have the GIL. For example, Jython (Python on the Java Virtual Machine) and IronPython (Python on the .NET framework) allow true multi-threading and better parallelism since they do not use the GIL.

These implementations do not have the same limitations as CPython and can execute multiple threads in parallel across multiple cores. However, they are less commonly used and may not support all CPython features or libraries.

When to Use Multi-threading in Python

I/O-bound Tasks: Python's threading module is still effective for handling I/O-bound tasks, where threads spend a lot of time waiting for input/output operations (e.g., web scraping, network services, file handling). In these cases, Python threads can work concurrently, allowing the program to remain responsive and perform multiple I/O operations simultaneously.

CPU-bound Tasks: For CPU-heavy tasks (e.g., scientific computing, simulations), multi-threading in CPython may not provide significant performance benefits due to the GIL. Instead, multiprocessing or using external libraries like NumPy (which leverages C for computation) can be more efficient.

Conclusion

The Global Interpreter Lock (GIL) in CPython is both a safeguard for thread safety and a limitation for parallel execution. While it simplifies memory management by ensuring only one thread runs Python bytecode at a time, it also means Python threads cannot fully utilize multiple CPU cores for CPU-bound tasks. Developers can still benefit from Python's threading model for I/O-bound tasks, but for CPU-bound tasks, techniques like multiprocessing or using external libraries are often necessary to achieve true parallelism. Understanding the GIL is crucial for optimizing Python programs in concurrent and parallel computing environments.

2.3. Workarounds for the GIL

While the Global Interpreter Lock (GIL) in CPython limits the parallel execution of threads in multi-core systems, there are several workarounds and strategies that developers can use to overcome the GIL's limitations and optimize Python programs for parallel processing. These workarounds primarily focus on utilizing multi-core systems for CPU-bound tasks or enhancing the concurrency of I/O-bound tasks.

1. Multiprocessing

The multiprocessing module is one of the most effective ways to bypass the GIL. Unlike threads, processes in Python run in their own memory space and have their own Python interpreter, meaning each process can run on a separate core and execute independently. Since each process has its own GIL, the limitation imposed by the GIL is avoided.

How It Works: Instead of using threads, you can use the multiprocessing module to spawn multiple processes. Each process runs in parallel, fully utilizing multiple CPU cores, thus enabling true parallelism.

Benefits:

True Parallelism: Since each process has its own GIL, processes can run concurrently across multiple CPU cores.
Avoids GIL: Computationally heavy tasks can be distributed across processes to bypass the GIL's bottleneck.

Drawbacks:

Higher Overhead: Processes have separate memory spaces, so inter-process communication (IPC) can be slower compared to threads, especially for tasks that need frequent data sharing.
Memory Usage: Each process has its own memory space, which can lead to higher memory consumption.

Example:

```python
Copy code
import multiprocessing

def compute_square(number):
    return number * number

if __name__ == "__main__":
    numbers = [1, 2, 3, 4, 5]
    with multiprocessing.Pool() as pool:
        results = pool.map(compute_square, numbers)
    print(results)
```

2. Cython and C Extensions

Cython is a superset of Python that allows you to write C-like code within Python. It can be used to bypass the GIL for performance-critical sections of code. By writing certain functions in C and compiling them, Cython allows Python code to run more efficiently, and it can also release the GIL when performing computations outside of Python's memory management.

How It Works: Cython lets you write C code inside Python functions, and during CPU-intensive operations, it can release the GIL, allowing true parallelism during the execution of C code.

Benefits:

Performance Boost: By writing performance-critical parts of the code in C, you can significantly improve performance.
GIL Release: Cython can release the GIL during CPU-bound operations, enabling parallelism.

Drawbacks:

Complexity: Writing and maintaining C code within Python can increase code complexity.

Dependency on Cython: You need to install Cython and compile the code, which can add steps to the development process.

Example (with Cython):

```cython
Copy code
# cython_example.pyx
cdef int compute_square(int number):
    return number * number
```

You can compile this using cythonize and use it within your Python code to speed up the computation.

3. Threading for I/O-bound Tasks

While the GIL limits the parallelism for CPU-bound tasks, it has less of an impact on I/O-bound tasks. When a thread performs I/O operations (such as waiting for data from the network or reading from a file), it releases the GIL, allowing other threads to execute in the meantime.

How It Works: Python's threading module is suitable for tasks where threads spend significant time waiting on I/O operations (e.g., file I/O, network I/O). While one thread is blocked on I/O, other threads can continue executing Python code.

Benefits:

Concurrency for I/O: Threads can perform I/O-bound operations concurrently, improving the performance of applications like web scrapers, network servers, or database applications.

Lower Memory Usage: Threads share the same memory space, so memory usage is generally lower compared to processes.

Drawbacks:

Limited Parallelism: For CPU-bound tasks, threading does not provide true parallelism due to the GIL.

Threads cannot fully utilize multiple CPU cores for heavy computations.

Example:

```python
Copy code
import threading
import time

def fetch_data_from_server():
    time.sleep(2)
    print("Data fetched")

threads = []
for _ in range(5):
    thread = threading.Thread(target=fetch_data_from_server)
    threads.append(thread)
    thread.start()

for thread in threads:
    thread.join()
```

4. Using External Libraries (NumPy, SciPy)

Many scientific and numerical libraries, such as NumPy and SciPy, are written in C or Fortran and can bypass the GIL during computation. These libraries handle heavy calculations outside the GIL's constraints, allowing true parallelism on multiple cores for numerical tasks.

How It Works: Libraries like NumPy perform low-level operations in C, which does not require Python bytecode execution. These libraries can release the GIL during heavy computations, enabling true parallel execution.

Benefits:

High Performance: Libraries like NumPy and SciPy are optimized for numerical computing, and their operations can be parallelized.
GIL Release: These libraries release the GIL during intensive computations, making them ideal for scientific

computations, machine learning, and other CPU-bound tasks.

Drawbacks:

Specialized Use: These libraries are designed for specific use cases, such as numerical computing, and are not applicable to all types of applications.

5. Alternative Python Implementations

Some Python implementations, like Jython (Python on the JVM) and IronPython (Python on the .NET framework), do not have a GIL and can perform multi-threading and parallelism more effectively on multi-core systems.

How It Works: These implementations do not use the GIL, so they can execute multiple threads simultaneously on different cores, providing true parallelism for both I/O-bound and CPU-bound tasks.

Benefits:

True Parallelism: These implementations can fully utilize multi-core processors without the limitations of the GIL.

Better Concurrency: For applications requiring high levels of concurrency, these implementations provide better performance.

Drawbacks:

Limited Ecosystem: These alternative implementations do not support all Python libraries and features, especially those relying on CPython-specific extensions.

Conclusion

While the GIL limits Python's multi-threading capabilities, especially for CPU-bound tasks, there are several workarounds that allow developers to achieve parallelism and improve performance. Strategies such as multiprocessing, Cython, and using external libraries like NumPy can help bypass the GIL for computationally intensive operations. For I/O-bound tasks, threading remains a viable option. For those needing full multi-core utilization, exploring alternative

Python implementations like Jython or IronPython can also be beneficial. Understanding when and how to use these workarounds is key to optimizing Python applications for concurrency and parallelism.

2.4. Using Multiprocessing to Bypass the GIL

The Global Interpreter Lock (GIL) in CPython severely limits the ability of multi-threaded programs to fully utilize multi-core processors, particularly for CPU-bound tasks. This is because the GIL ensures that only one thread can execute Python bytecode at a time, preventing true parallel execution in multi-threaded programs. One of the most effective ways to bypass the

GIL and achieve true parallelism is by using the multiprocessing module.

What is Multiprocessing?

The multiprocessing module allows you to create separate processes, each with its own memory space and Python interpreter. Since each process has its own GIL, multiple processes can run concurrently on different CPU cores, allowing Python to achieve true parallelism.

Unlike threads, which share the same memory space, processes run in isolated memory spaces and communicate with each other via inter-process communication (IPC) mechanisms, such as pipes, queues, or shared memory. This means that each process can execute independently, allowing Python programs to utilize multi-core systems for CPU-bound tasks.

How Multiprocessing Bypasses the GIL

Separate Memory Space: Each process created by the multiprocessing module has its own memory space. This means that processes do not share the same memory, so the GIL does not need to synchronize access to shared memory.

Independent Python Interpreters: Since each process has its own Python interpreter and GIL, they can run Python code concurrently. This avoids the GIL's bottleneck and allows true parallel execution across multiple CPU cores.

True Parallelism: Unlike threads, which are limited by the GIL, processes in Python can run on different CPU cores, fully utilizing the available processing power and improving performance for CPU-bound tasks.

Benefits of Using Multiprocessing

Full Utilization of Multi-Core Processors:

Multiprocessing allows Python programs to fully utilize multi-core systems. Each process can run on a separate core, enabling parallel execution of CPU-intensive tasks, such as complex computations, simulations, or data processing.

Avoidance of GIL:

By using processes instead of threads, the GIL is bypassed. Each process has its own GIL and memory space, which means the program can perform multiple tasks in parallel without being restricted by the GIL. Increased Performance for CPU-bound Tasks:

CPU-bound tasks, such as mathematical calculations, image processing, or data analysis, can benefit significantly from multiprocessing. By splitting the workload across multiple processes, Python can make use of all available CPU cores, leading to a performance boost.

Isolation and Safety:

Since each process runs independently, there is no risk of data corruption due to concurrent access, unlike in multi-threading where shared memory requires careful management (e.g., locks or synchronization).

Drawbacks of Multiprocessing

Higher Memory Usage:

Each process has its own memory space, so memory usage can increase significantly compared to multi-threading, where threads share the same memory. This is especially important when dealing with large data sets or running many processes concurrently.

Inter-process Communication (IPC):

Since processes do not share memory, communication between them requires mechanisms like queues, pipes, or shared memory, which can introduce overhead and complexity.
IPC can be slower than thread communication because of the need to transfer data between separate memory spaces.

Increased Overhead:

Creating and managing multiple processes introduces additional overhead compared to using threads. This overhead includes process creation time, memory allocation, and context switching between processes.
For smaller tasks, the overhead of multiprocessing may outweigh the benefits.

Example of Using Multiprocessing

Here's an example of how you can use the multiprocessing module to parallelize a CPU-bound task, such as calculating the square of numbers, and bypass the GIL:

```python
Copy code
import multiprocessing

def compute_square(number):
    return number * number
```

```python
if __name__ == "__main__":
    numbers = [1, 2, 3, 4, 5]

    # Create a Pool of processes to parallelize the task
    with multiprocessing.Pool() as pool:
        results = pool.map(compute_square, numbers)

    print(results)
```

Explanation:

The Pool() creates a pool of worker processes, which can process multiple tasks in parallel.

The pool.map() function maps the compute_square function to each number in the numbers list, distributing the work across the available processes in the pool.

Since each process has its own GIL, the task is executed concurrently on multiple CPU cores, achieving true parallelism and bypassing the GIL.

Sharing Data Between Processes

To share data between processes, you can use shared memory or queues. For example, here's how you can use a Queue for inter-process communication:

python
Copy code
```
import multiprocessing

def compute_square(number, queue):
    result = number * number
    queue.put(result)  # Put the result in the queue

if __name__ == "__main__":
    numbers = [1, 2, 3, 4, 5]
    queue = multiprocessing.Queue()

    processes = []
    for number in numbers:
                                process = multiprocessing.Process(target=compute_square, args=(number, queue))
        processes.append(process)
```

```
    process.start()

for process in processes:
    process.join()

results = []
while not queue.empty():
    results.append(queue.get())

print(results)
```

Explanation:

Each process computes the square of a number and places the result into the queue.
After all processes finish, the main process collects the results from the queue.

When to Use Multiprocessing

CPU-bound Tasks:

Use multiprocessing for tasks that are computationally intensive and require significant processing power, such as scientific calculations, data analysis, image processing, or machine learning model training.
It is ideal when tasks can be divided into independent sub-tasks that can run concurrently.

Large Data Processing:

When dealing with large datasets or time-consuming operations that can be parallelized, multiprocessing can provide a significant performance boost.

True Parallelism:

If you need true parallelism to fully utilize multi-core processors, multiprocessing is the go-to solution. It allows you to bypass the GIL and distribute workloads across CPU cores.

Conclusion

The multiprocessing module in Python is a powerful tool to achieve true parallelism and bypass the Global Interpreter Lock (GIL), particularly for CPU-bound tasks. By using multiple processes instead of threads, Python can leverage multi-core processors and improve performance for computationally heavy operations. While multiprocessing can introduce additional complexity, such as memory overhead and inter-process communication, it is the best approach for utilizing the full potential of multi-core systems in Python.

Chapter 3
Threading in Python

Threading in Python allows for concurrent execution of code within a single process, where multiple threads share the same memory space. This is useful for performing multiple tasks at the same time without creating separate processes, reducing overhead and memory usage compared to process-based parallelism. Python's threading module provides a way to work with threads.

How Threading Works in Python

.Threads in a Single Process: A thread is a separate flow of execution within a program. Multiple threads within the same process share the same memory space, which makes inter-thread communication easier but also requires careful synchronization to avoid data corruption.

Concurrency, Not Parallelism: Python threads are primarily used for concurrent tasks, such as handling multiple I/O operations, rather than for parallel execution of CPU-bound tasks. This is because of Python's Global Interpreter Lock (GIL), which allows only one thread to execute Python bytecode at a time.

GIL and Threading: The Global Interpreter Lock (GIL) in CPython limits true parallelism for CPU-bound tasks. However, for I/O-bound tasks (such as reading from a disk, network communication, or waiting for user input), the GIL is released while waiting for external resources, allowing other threads to run concurrently and improving performance.

Benefits of Threading

Concurrency: Threading allows a program to handle multiple tasks concurrently, making it efficient for I/O-bound applications like web servers, network services, or database handling.

Lower Memory Usage: Since threads share the same memory space, using threads is more memory-efficient than spawning multiple processes, which require separate memory for each process.

Simplified Communication: Threads share the same address space, making it easier for them to communicate and share data compared to processes.

Challenges of Threading

GIL Limitation: For CPU-bound tasks, threading does not provide true parallelism because the GIL allows only one thread to execute Python bytecode at a time, limiting the ability to fully utilize multi-core processors.

Synchronization: Threads need to be synchronized to prevent issues like data corruption when multiple threads access shared resources. This requires using locks, semaphores, or other synchronization mechanisms.

Example of Threading in Python

```python
Copy code
import threading
import time

def print_numbers():
    for i in range(5):
        print(i)
```

```
    time.sleep(1)

def print_letters():
    for letter in 'ABCDE':
        print(letter)
        time.sleep(1)

# Create two threads
thread1 = threading.Thread(target=print_numbers)
thread2 = threading.Thread(target=print_letters)

# Start the threads
thread1.start()
thread2.start()

# Wait for both threads to finish
thread1.join()
thread2.join()

print("Both threads finished execution.")
```

In this example, two threads run concurrently, printing numbers and letters. While one thread waits (sleeps) for a second, the other can continue execution, showcasing the concurrency that threading provides.

When to Use Threading

I/O-bound tasks: Threading is ideal for tasks that involve waiting for external resources (e.g., file I/O, network requests, user input), where threads can perform useful work while waiting.

Multitasking in a Single Program: Threading is suitable for applications that need to perform multiple operations at once but do not require heavy CPU computation, such as web scraping, monitoring, or real-time data processing.

Conclusion

Threading in Python is a powerful tool for handling concurrency, especially for I/O-bound tasks, allowing for efficient multitasking in a single process. However, due to the GIL, Python threads are limited in terms of true parallel execution for CPU-bound tasks, making other approaches like multiprocessing more suitable for CPU-heavy workloads. Nonetheless, threading remains a key technique for improving performance in many types of Python applications.

3.1. Introduction to Threads in Python

In Python, a thread is the smallest unit of a CPU's execution. A thread represents a single flow of control within a process. Threads in Python enable concurrent execution of tasks, allowing a program to perform multiple operations at the same time. This is particularly useful for tasks like handling multiple I/O operations, where threads can wait for external resources without blocking the main execution flow.

The Python threading module provides a way to work with threads, making it easier to create and manage them. Threads run within a single process and share the same memory space, which can be beneficial for sharing data between tasks but also requires careful synchronization to avoid issues like race conditions.

Key Concepts

Process vs. Thread:

A process is an independent program that runs in its own memory space, while a thread is a smaller unit of a process that shares memory and resources with other threads within the same process.
A process is more isolated, whereas threads are lighter and have less overhead due to shared memory space.

Concurrency:

Threading is typically used for concurrent execution, where multiple tasks can be performed simultaneously. However, this does not necessarily mean tasks are run in parallel on separate cores (as threading in Python is limited by the Global Interpreter Lock (GIL)).

For I/O-bound tasks, threading is ideal as it allows other threads to continue running while one is waiting on external I/O operations.

Global Interpreter Lock (GIL):

The GIL is a mechanism in CPython (the standard Python implementation) that ensures only one thread can execute Python bytecode at a time. While this is not a limitation for I/O-bound tasks (because threads release the GIL while waiting for I/O), it does limit true parallelism for CPU-bound tasks.

In CPU-bound tasks, the GIL prevents threads from fully utilizing multi-core processors, and hence, Python threads may not achieve significant speed-up in these cases.

Creating Threads in Python

The threading module provides a simple and straightforward way to create threads. You can create threads by subclassing the Thread class or by passing a target function to a Thread object.

Here's an example of creating threads using the threading module:

```python
Copy code
import threading
import time

# Function to be executed by the thread
def print_numbers():
    for i in range(5):
        print(i)
        time.sleep(1)

def print_letters():
    for letter in 'ABCDE':
        print(letter)
        time.sleep(1)

# Create threads
thread1 = threading.Thread(target=print_numbers)
thread2 = threading.Thread(target=print_letters)
```

```
# Start the threads
thread1.start()
thread2.start()

# Wait for both threads to finish
thread1.join()
thread2.join()

print("Both threads finished execution.")
```

Thread Lifecycle

Creation: A thread is created by initializing a Thread object. The target function (or method) to be executed by the thread is passed during initialization.

Starting: The start() method is called to begin the execution of the thread. This will invoke the target function in a new thread of execution.

Joining: The join() method ensures that the main program waits for the thread to complete before continuing. If you call join() on a thread, the program will pause until that thread finishes its task.

Termination: A thread terminates when the target function has completed its execution. Threads can be forced to stop using daemon threads or other mechanisms, but this is generally not recommended due to the risk of leaving shared resources in an inconsistent state.

Thread Synchronization

Since threads share the same memory space, you must synchronize access to shared data to prevent race conditions. Python provides several synchronization tools to help with this:

Locks: threading.Lock is used to prevent multiple threads from accessing a shared resource at the same time.

RLocks (Reentrant Locks):

threading.RLock is similar to Lock but allows a thread to acquire the lock multiple times without causing a deadlock.

Semaphores and Conditions: These are used for more complex synchronization between threads.

Example of using a lock:

```python
Copy code
import threading

lock = threading.Lock()

def safe_increment(counter):
    with lock:
        # Critical section
        counter[0] += 1
        print(counter[0])

counter = [0]  # Shared resource

# Create threads
```

```
threads = []
for _ in range(5):
    thread = threading.Thread(target=safe_increment,
args=(counter,))
  threads.append(thread)
  thread.start()

# Wait for all threads to finish
for thread in threads:
  thread.join()

print("Final counter value:", counter[0])
```

In this example, a lock is used to ensure that only one thread can modify the shared counter at a time.

When to Use Threading

I/O-bound Tasks: Threading is best for programs that spend a significant amount of time waiting for external I/O operations, such as web servers, network clients, or database queries.

Multitasking: Threading is useful when you need to perform multiple tasks simultaneously within a single program, such as updating a UI while processing data or handling multiple requests concurrently.

Parallelism in Limited Cases: Threading can still be useful in scenarios where the threads are mostly I/O-bound and can benefit from concurrency, even if Python doesn't provide true parallelism due to the GIL.

Conclusion

Threads in Python are an essential tool for enabling concurrency in programs, allowing tasks to be performed simultaneously without the overhead of creating separate processes. While CPU-bound tasks may not benefit significantly from threading due to the GIL, I/O-bound tasks can still see substantial performance gains by allowing threads to handle multiple I/O operations concurrently. Python's threading module provides a simple interface for creating and managing threads, with synchronization tools to manage shared resources safely. For tasks that need true parallelism on multi-core processors, alternatives like multiprocessing may be more suitable.

3.2. The Threading Module: Basics

The threading module in Python provides a way to run multiple threads (independent flows of execution) concurrently in a program. Threads are lightweight and share the same memory space, allowing them to communicate and share data easily. Python's threading module provides tools to manage and synchronize threads, making it easier to perform multitasking.

Here are the key concepts and components of the threading module:

1. Creating Threads

The most basic way to create a thread in Python is by using the Thread class from the threading module. You can create a thread by either subclassing Thread and overriding the run() method or by passing a target function to the Thread object.

Example: Creating a Thread
python
Copy code

```python
import threading
import time

def print_numbers():
    for i in range(5):
        print(i)
        time.sleep(1)

# Create a thread and pass the target function
thread = threading.Thread(target=print_numbers)

# Start the thread
thread.start()
```

```
# Wait for the thread to finish
thread.join()

print("Thread execution complete.")
```

In this example:

target=print_numbers specifies the function to be executed by the thread.
start() begins the thread's execution.
join() ensures the main program waits for the thread to finish before continuing.

2. Thread Lifecycle

The lifecycle of a thread includes the following states:

New: A thread has been created but hasn't started execution.

Started: A thread has been started by calling start(), and its target function is executing.

Stopped: A thread has finished its execution, either because its target function has completed or it was explicitly terminated.

Example of Thread Lifecycle:
python
Copy code

```python
import threading

def simple_task():
    print("Task started")
    # Simulating some work
    time.sleep(2)
    print("Task finished")

# Create the thread
task_thread = threading.Thread(target=simple_task)

print("Thread is in 'New' state.")
task_thread.start()  # Move thread to 'Started' state
print("Thread is in 'Started' state.")
```

```
task_thread.join()   # Wait for thread to finish (move to
'Stopped' state)
print("Thread is in 'Stopped' state.")
```

3. Thread Synchronization

Since threads share the same memory space, you must carefully manage access to shared resources to avoid race conditions or inconsistent data. Python provides several synchronization tools for this purpose:

Locks: The most basic synchronization tool. A lock allows only one thread to access a critical section at a time.

RLocks: Reentrant locks allow a thread to acquire the lock multiple times without causing a deadlock.

Semaphores: Used to manage access to a shared resource with limited capacity.

Events: Used for thread synchronization where one thread signals one or more threads to continue execution.

Example: Using a Lock
python
Copy code
```
import threading

# Shared resource
counter = 0

# Lock for synchronization
lock = threading.Lock()

def increment():
    global counter
    with lock:
        # Critical section
        counter += 1
        print(f"Counter: {counter}")

# Create multiple threads
```

```
threads = []
for _ in range(5):
    thread = threading.Thread(target=increment)
    threads.append(thread)
    thread.start()

# Wait for all threads to finish
for thread in threads:
    thread.join()

print("Final counter value:", counter)
```
In this example, the lock is used to ensure that only one thread can modify the shared counter at a time, preventing race conditions.

4. Threading with Arguments

You can pass arguments to the target function of a thread using the args parameter in the Thread constructor. This is useful when the target function requires arguments.

Example: Passing Arguments to a Thread

```python
Copy code
import threading

def print_message(message):
    print(f"Message: {message}")

# Create a thread and pass an argument
thread = threading.Thread(target=print_message,
args=("Hello, World!",))

thread.start()
thread.join()
```

Here, args=("Hello, World!",) passes the argument to the print_message function.

5. Daemon Threads

A daemon thread is a thread that runs in the background and does not prevent the program from exiting. When the main program exits, daemon threads are abruptly stopped.

Daemon threads are useful for background tasks that are not critical to the program's operation, such as logging, monitoring, or cleanup tasks.

Example: Daemon Threads
python
Copy code
```python
import threading
import time

def background_task():
    while True:
        print("Daemon thread running...")
        time.sleep(1)

# Create a daemon thread
daemon_thread = threading.Thread(target=background_task)
daemon_thread.daemon = True  # Set the thread as a daemon

daemon_thread.start()
```

```python
# Main program will exit after 5 seconds
time.sleep(5)
print("Main program exiting...")
```

In this example, the daemon thread runs in the background, printing messages, but the program exits after 5 seconds, terminating the daemon thread.

6. Thread Pooling

Thread pooling is a technique where a fixed number of threads are created and used for executing multiple tasks. The concurrent.futures.ThreadPoolExecutor is a higher-level API for managing thread pools in Python.

Example: Using ThreadPoolExecutor
python
Copy code

```python
from concurrent.futures import ThreadPoolExecutor

def print_square(number):
    print(f"Square of {number} is {number**2}")
```

```
# Create a ThreadPoolExecutor with 3 threads
with ThreadPoolExecutor(max_workers=3) as executor:
    executor.map(print_square, [1, 2, 3, 4, 5])
```

This approach simplifies managing a pool of threads to execute multiple tasks concurrently.

Conclusion

The threading module in Python provides an easy-to-use interface for creating and managing threads. By using threads, you can perform concurrent execution within a single process, making it useful for I/O-bound tasks and scenarios where you need to perform multiple tasks simultaneously. However, threading comes with challenges like synchronization and the limitations imposed by the Global Interpreter Lock (GIL), which affects CPU-bound tasks. By understanding the basics of creating, synchronizing, and managing threads, you can efficiently use Python's threading capabilities for a variety of applications.

3.3. Managing Threads: Synchronization and Deadlocks

In Python, when using threads, synchronization and deadlocks are key concepts that need to be understood to ensure that multiple threads can safely work with shared resources without causing errors or unpredictable behavior. Since threads in Python run concurrently and share the same memory space, synchronization mechanisms are crucial to avoid issues like race conditions, data corruption, or deadlocks.

1. Thread Synchronization

Thread synchronization is the process of ensuring that threads properly coordinate access to shared resources to prevent conflicts or data corruption.

Synchronization ensures that only one thread can access a shared resource at a time, which is particularly important in multi-threaded applications.

The most common synchronization mechanisms in Python are locks, RLocks, semaphores, and events. These are all part of the threading module.

a) Locks

A lock is the simplest synchronization primitive. When a thread acquires a lock, other threads trying to acquire the same lock are blocked until the lock is released.

A critical section is a part of the program where shared resources are accessed. Locks ensure that only one thread can enter the critical section at a time, avoiding race conditions.

Example: Using Locks
python
Copy code
```python
import threading

counter = 0
lock = threading.Lock()
```

```python
def increment():
    global counter
    with lock:  # Acquire lock
        counter += 1
        print(f"Counter: {counter}")

# Create multiple threads
threads = []
for _ in range(5):
    thread = threading.Thread(target=increment)
    threads.append(thread)
    thread.start()

# Wait for all threads to finish
for thread in threads:
    thread.join()

print("Final counter value:", counter)
```

In this example:

The lock ensures that only one thread can access the increment() function at a time, preventing race conditions where multiple threads might attempt to modify counter simultaneously.

b) RLocks (Reentrant Locks)

An RLock (reentrant lock) is a lock that allows a thread to acquire the same lock multiple times without causing a deadlock. This is useful when a thread needs to enter a critical section multiple times without releasing the lock in between.

Example: Using RLocks
python
Copy code

```python
import threading

lock = threading.RLock()

def recursive_task(level):
    with lock:
        print(f"Entering level {level}")
```

```
if level > 0:
    recursive_task(level - 1)
print(f"Exiting level {level}")
```

```
# Create a thread that uses the RLock
thread       =       threading.Thread(target=recursive_task,
args=(3,))
thread.start()
thread.join()
```

In this example, the thread can safely acquire the RLock multiple times within the recursive_task() function without causing a deadlock.

c) Semaphores

A semaphore controls access to a shared resource by limiting the number of threads that can access the resource simultaneously. It works like a counter that is decremented when a thread acquires the semaphore and incremented when a thread releases it.

Example: Using Semaphores

```python
Copy code
import threading
import time

semaphore = threading.Semaphore(2)  # Allow only 2 threads to access the resource

def access_resource(thread_id):
        print(f"Thread {thread_id} is waiting for the resource.")
    with semaphore:  # Acquire semaphore
        print(f"Thread {thread_id} is using the resource.")
        time.sleep(2)  # Simulate work with the resource
    print(f"Thread {thread_id} is releasing the resource.")

# Create and start multiple threads
threads = []
for i in range(5):
        thread = threading.Thread(target=access_resource, args=(i,))
    threads.append(thread)
    thread.start()
```

```
# Wait for all threads to finish
for thread in threads:
    thread.join()
```

In this example, the semaphore allows only two threads to access the shared resource at the same time, limiting concurrency and preventing resource contention.

d) Events

An event is a simple synchronization primitive that allows one thread to signal one or more threads to proceed with execution. Events are useful for coordinating the flow of multiple threads.

Example: Using Events
python
Copy code
```python
import threading

event = threading.Event()
```

```python
def wait_for_event():
    print("Thread is waiting for the event.")
    event.wait()  # Wait until the event is set
    print("Thread is proceeding after event is set.")

# Create and start threads
threads = []
for _ in range(3):
    thread = threading.Thread(target=wait_for_event)
    threads.append(thread)
    thread.start()

# Set the event after 2 seconds
import time
time.sleep(2)
print("Setting the event.")
event.set()

# Wait for all threads to finish
for thread in threads:
    thread.join()
```

In this example, the threads wait for the event to be set before proceeding. The event.set() method is called after a delay to release all waiting threads.

2. Deadlocks in Threading

A deadlock occurs when two or more threads are blocked forever, each waiting for the other to release a resource. This often happens when threads acquire multiple locks in different orders, leading to a circular dependency.

Example of Deadlock
python
Copy code
```python
import threading

lock1 = threading.Lock()
lock2 = threading.Lock()

def task1():
    with lock1:
        print("Task 1 acquired lock 1.")
```

```
    time.sleep(1)  # Simulate work
    with lock2:
        print("Task 1 acquired lock 2.")

def task2():
    with lock2:
        print("Task 2 acquired lock 2.")
        time.sleep(1)  # Simulate work
        with lock1:
            print("Task 2 acquired lock 1.")

# Create and start threads
thread1 = threading.Thread(target=task1)
thread2 = threading.Thread(target=task2)

thread1.start()
thread2.start()

thread1.join()
thread2.join()
```

In this example, task1 acquires lock1 and waits for lock2, while task2 acquires lock2 and waits for lock1.

This leads to a deadlock because both threads are waiting for the other to release a lock.

Preventing Deadlocks

Lock Ordering: Always acquire locks in a fixed order. If multiple threads need multiple locks, make sure they always acquire them in the same order to avoid circular dependencies.

Timeouts: Use timeouts to avoid threads waiting indefinitely for locks. You can use lock.acquire(timeout=seconds) to limit how long a thread will wait for a lock.

Deadlock Detection: Some systems implement algorithms to detect deadlocks and prevent them by forcibly terminating one of the threads.

3. Best Practices for Synchronization

Minimize Locking: Only lock the critical section of code that truly needs synchronization. Avoid locking large portions of code to reduce the chance of contention and deadlocks.

Use Higher-Level Constructs: Python's concurrent.futures module provides high-level abstractions like ThreadPoolExecutor that manage synchronization automatically.

Monitor Resource Usage: Keep track of the resources each thread holds and avoid circular dependencies in locking.

Conclusion

Thread synchronization is essential when multiple threads share data or resources, and the threading module provides various synchronization primitives like locks, RLocks, semaphores, and events to help manage access to shared resources. Proper synchronization ensures data integrity and prevents issues like race conditions and deadlocks. By following best practices and carefully managing how threads acquire locks, you can build efficient, thread-safe multi-threaded applications in Python.

3.4. When to Use Threading in Python

Threading in Python allows multiple tasks to be executed concurrently within the same process, offering a way to make programs more efficient, particularly for certain types of workloads. However, not all problems can benefit from threading, so it's important to understand when and why to use threading in Python. Below are some scenarios where threading can be useful:

1. I/O-Bound Tasks

Threading is particularly effective for I/O-bound tasks. These are tasks that spend a significant amount of time waiting for external resources, such as reading from or writing to files, making network requests, or querying a database.

In I/O-bound tasks, the thread often has to wait for an operation to complete, such as downloading data or reading data from a disk. During this waiting time, the thread releases the Global Interpreter Lock (GIL) in CPython, allowing other threads to run and perform useful work.

Examples of I/O-Bound Tasks:

Downloading files from a web server.
Reading and writing to a file or database.
Making HTTP requests to external APIs.
Waiting for user input or interacting with an external device.

Example: Threading for I/O Operations
python
Copy code
import threading

```python
import time

def download_file(file_url):
    print(f"Downloading {file_url}...")
    time.sleep(2)  # Simulate download time
    print(f"Downloaded {file_url}")

# List of file URLs to download
file_urls = ["file1.txt", "file2.txt", "file3.txt"]

threads = []
for url in file_urls:
    thread = threading.Thread(target=download_file, args=(url,))
    threads.append(thread)
    thread.start()

# Wait for all threads to finish
for thread in threads:
    thread.join()

print("All downloads completed.")
```

In this example, the threads perform I/O-bound operations (downloading files), and threading allows them to run concurrently, significantly reducing the overall time for all downloads to complete.

2. Concurrency in Programs with Multiple Tasks

Threading is useful when your program needs to perform multiple tasks simultaneously or concurrently without the overhead of creating multiple processes. This could involve handling multiple tasks like updating the user interface, processing data, or monitoring inputs simultaneously.

Examples:

GUI applications: You may need a background thread to handle long-running tasks like data processing while keeping the user interface responsive.
Web servers: A multi-threaded server can handle multiple client requests concurrently.

Example: Threading for Concurrent Tasks

```python
Copy code
import threading
import time

def task1():
    print("Starting task 1")
    time.sleep(3)
    print("Task 1 completed")

def task2():
    print("Starting task 2")
    time.sleep(2)
    print("Task 2 completed")

# Create threads for concurrent tasks
thread1 = threading.Thread(target=task1)
thread2 = threading.Thread(target=task2)

# Start threads
thread1.start()
thread2.start()
```

```
# Wait for both threads to finish
thread1.join()
thread2.join()

print("Both tasks completed.")
```

In this example, task1 and task2 are executed concurrently, allowing them to complete faster than if they were executed sequentially.

3. Multitasking in Long-Running Applications

If your application needs to perform multiple long-running operations, threading can be helpful in preventing it from becoming unresponsive. By breaking down tasks into smaller, independent units of work (each executed in a separate thread), the program can remain responsive while working on background tasks.

For instance:

A program that reads sensor data while also processing incoming network requests.

An application that monitors for events while running long computations.

4. Handling High Throughput in Network Servers

In network servers, multiple clients may need to be handled simultaneously. Threading is often used to handle multiple network requests concurrently, allowing the server to process each request in its own thread.

Web servers, chat servers, and other networked services benefit from threading to ensure that each client gets a fast response. However, thread pooling may be preferred in high-load situations to avoid excessive resource consumption from creating too many threads.

Example: Threading in Network Servers

```python
Copy code
import threading
import socket
```

```python
def handle_client(client_socket):
    print("Client connected")
    message = client_socket.recv(1024)
    print(f"Received message: {message}")
    client_socket.send(b"Hello, Client!")
    client_socket.close()


server = socket.socket(socket.AF_INET,
socket.SOCK_STREAM)
server.bind(("localhost", 8080))
server.listen(5)

print("Server is listening on port 8080...")

while True:
    client_socket, addr = server.accept()
    # Handle each client in a separate thread
    client_thread = threading.Thread(target=handle_client,
args=(client_socket,))
    client_thread.start()
```

Here, the server listens for incoming client connections and uses threading to handle each client request in a separate thread, allowing for efficient, concurrent handling of multiple clients.

5. Improving Program Responsiveness (User Interfaces)

In user interface (UI) applications, threading is often used to ensure the UI remains responsive while performing time-consuming tasks in the background.

For example, in desktop applications using Tkinter or PyQt, threading can be used to process data or perform tasks in the background while ensuring the UI can continue to update and interact with the user.

Without threading, a UI might freeze or become unresponsive while executing long-running tasks. Threading helps to maintain interactivity during such operations.

Example: Threading in a GUI Application (Tkinter)
python

```
Copy code
import threading
import tkinter as tk
import time

def long_running_task():
    time.sleep(5)
    print("Task Completed")

def start_task():
    # Create a thread to run the long-running task
    thread = threading.Thread(target=long_running_task)
    thread.start()

# Set up the Tkinter GUI
root = tk.Tk()
root.title("Threading Example")

start_button = tk.Button(root, text="Start Task",
command=start_task)
start_button.pack()

root.mainloop()
```

In this example, clicking the "Start Task" button triggers a long-running task, which runs in a separate thread, allowing the GUI to remain responsive.

6. Avoiding Blocking Operations

Threading can be used to avoid blocking operations in a program. For example, when a program must wait for data from an external source, threading allows other tasks to continue running during the wait. This is useful in applications that require non-blocking behavior, such as continuously polling data sources or maintaining a real-time feed.

When Not to Use Threading in Python

While threading can be powerful, it's not always the right solution. In some cases, multiprocessing might be more appropriate, especially when tasks are CPU-bound. This is because Python's Global Interpreter Lock (GIL) can prevent threads from executing Python bytecode in parallel on multi-core processors, limiting performance for CPU-bound tasks.

When to Consider Alternatives:

CPU-Bound Tasks: For tasks that require heavy computation, consider using multiprocessing instead of threading. The multiprocessing module can utilize multiple CPU cores by running separate processes, avoiding the GIL's limitations.
Complexity of Synchronization: If the synchronization of threads becomes too complex or error-prone, a different approach, such as using asyncio for asynchronous programming, may be a better choice.

Conclusion

Threading is an effective tool for achieving concurrency and improving the performance of I/O-bound or concurrent tasks in Python. It is especially beneficial in scenarios where tasks involve waiting for external resources (like files, network operations, or databases), improving program responsiveness and efficiency. However, threading is not suitable for CPU-bound tasks due to the GIL in CPython, and for those tasks, multiprocessing or asyncio might be more appropriate. As with any concurrent programming technique, it is important to carefully manage synchronization and avoid pitfalls such as deadlocks and race conditions.

3.5. Real-World Applications of Threading

Threading in Python is widely used in real-world applications to enhance the performance and responsiveness of programs. By allowing multiple tasks to be executed concurrently within the same process, threading makes it possible to handle multiple operations at once without blocking the program's execution. Below are several examples of real-world applications where threading is commonly used:

1. Web Servers

Web servers often need to handle multiple client requests concurrently. Each client typically interacts with the server via a network request, and the server must respond to each request. By using threading, web servers can manage multiple clients simultaneously without waiting for one request to complete before starting another.

For instance, a multi-threaded web server creates a new thread for each client request, ensuring that each client gets an immediate response, improving the server's overall efficiency and responsiveness.

Example:

Flask or Django with Threaded Server: Web frameworks like Flask and Django often use threading for handling multiple web requests concurrently, allowing each HTTP request to be processed in a separate thread.
Apache HTTP Server: The Apache server uses threading to handle multiple requests concurrently.

2. Chat Applications

In real-time communication applications like chat systems, threading is commonly used to manage simultaneous messages, notifications, and user interactions. Each user's input and output can be handled in a separate thread, which allows the application to send and receive messages concurrently without blocking the user's interface.

For example, in a multi-user chat system, a separate thread can be created for each user to handle the messages they send and receive, ensuring that one user's activity does not block or delay others.

Example:

Slack-like Apps: Multi-threaded chat systems, where each message or user interaction is handled in a separate thread, allowing for simultaneous conversations without any lag.

Real-Time Messaging Servers: Many real-time messaging servers, such as chatbots, use threading to interact with multiple clients at once, sending responses without delay.

3. Download Managers

Download managers are applications that handle multiple file downloads concurrently. These programs typically download files from the internet, often from multiple sources, and need to manage several ongoing downloads at the same time. By using threading, each file can be downloaded in its own thread, reducing the overall time needed to download multiple files.

Example:
Internet Download Managers (IDM): These programs often use threading to download multiple parts of a file concurrently, improving download speed. Multiple threads can also handle various files simultaneously, making the application efficient.

4. File Processing and Data ETL Pipelines

In data processing applications, threading can be used to process multiple files or data chunks concurrently. For instance, an ETL (Extract, Transform, Load) pipeline often deals with large datasets that need to be transformed or loaded into a database. By using threading, data can be processed in parallel, reducing the overall time required for the transformation.

Threading can be used for various stages of data processing, such as extracting data from multiple sources, transforming the data, and loading it into a database.

Example:

Log File Analysis: In a large system that generates logs, threading can be used to analyze multiple log files in parallel, identifying patterns, errors, or incidents faster than processing each file sequentially.

Data Scraping: When scraping data from multiple websites, threading helps speed up the process by handling requests concurrently.

5. GUI Applications

Graphical User Interface (GUI) applications benefit from threading to ensure the user interface remains responsive while executing long-running tasks in the background. Without threading, a long-running task such as downloading files, processing data, or making network requests could freeze the UI, making it unresponsive to user actions.

Threading allows background tasks to run in separate threads, so the main thread can continue to update the GUI and respond to user input.

Example:

Text Editors or IDEs: When compiling code or running a build process in an IDE (e.g., Visual Studio Code or

PyCharm), threading can be used to run the build in the background while the user continues to work with the editor.

Data Visualization Apps: Data visualization apps often process large datasets. Threading ensures the main UI thread remains responsive while the data processing occurs in the background.

6. Real-Time Data Processing Systems

Real-time systems, such as those found in financial services, healthcare, or IoT (Internet of Things), often require the ability to process and analyze data as it is generated or received. For example, a financial market monitoring system needs to analyze and process multiple streams of data (e.g., stock prices, news feeds, social media sentiment) concurrently to detect trends and respond to market changes in real time.

Threading is commonly used to handle multiple data streams concurrently, ensuring the system remains responsive and efficient.

Example:

Stock Market Monitoring Systems: A stock trading application can use threading to manage multiple stock price feeds concurrently, allowing traders to receive real-time updates for multiple stocks without delay.

Sensor Data Collection: In IoT applications, threads are used to manage the concurrent collection and processing of data from multiple sensors, ensuring that each sensor's data is processed in real time.

7. Machine Learning and AI Training

In machine learning and AI training, especially for deep learning models, threading can be used to parallelize data preprocessing and model training tasks. Training machine learning models often involves working with large datasets, and threading can help speed up data loading, transformation, and even distributed model training. Although multiprocessing is often more commonly used for CPU-bound tasks like training large models, threading can still play a role in parallelizing operations that involve I/O-bound tasks, like reading data from disk or querying databases.

Example:

Data Augmentation: In deep learning, threading can be used to apply data augmentation techniques (e.g., rotating, scaling images) in parallel to increase the dataset size and accelerate training.
Data Loading: Threading can be used to load large datasets into memory for batch processing during training, avoiding bottlenecks in data availability.

8. Networking Applications

Networking applications that require continuous or real-time interaction with multiple systems or devices can benefit from threading. For example, a network monitoring tool or a service that continuously receives packets from multiple clients may use threading to handle each connection in a separate thread. This allows the application to interact with many devices concurrently without blocking on any one device.

Example:

Network Monitoring Tools: Network monitoring systems use threading to concurrently process and analyze network traffic from multiple sources, providing real-time insights into network health and performance.

Web Scrapers: Web scraping tools often use threading to send concurrent requests to multiple web pages, speeding up the scraping process and reducing total execution time.

9. Simulations and Modeling

Simulations that model real-world systems (e.g., weather patterns, traffic flow, financial models) often involve running many independent calculations or agents concurrently. Threading can be used to parallelize these calculations, allowing a simulation to run faster and with higher scalability.

Example:

Physics Simulations: In scientific computing, simulations of complex physical systems (e.g., climate simulations, particle physics) can be parallelized using threading to distribute the computation across multiple threads.

Traffic Simulation: Traffic management systems that model the movement of vehicles through a city can use threading to simulate the interactions of individual vehicles concurrently.

10. Games and Game Engines

Games often use threading to handle different game subsystems, such as graphics rendering, physics simulations, AI behaviors, and network communication, simultaneously. Threading allows each subsystem to operate independently, ensuring smooth gameplay and responsiveness.

Example:

Game Engines: In game development, threading is used to update the physics engine, process player inputs, and render graphics concurrently, all while keeping the game responsive and immersive.

Conclusion

Threading plays a critical role in a wide range of real-world applications, enabling concurrent execution of tasks that improve performance, responsiveness, and scalability. From web servers and networking tools to machine learning systems and real-time data processing, threading helps manage multiple tasks concurrently without blocking the main program. However, it's important to carefully design threading mechanisms to avoid common pitfalls such as race conditions and deadlocks. When used appropriately, threading can significantly enhance the efficiency and user experience of complex applications.

Chapter 4
Multiprocessing for Concurrency

Multiprocessing is a Python programming technique that allows programs to achieve concurrency by creating multiple processes, each running independently. Unlike threading, which operates within a single process, multiprocessing leverages multiple processes to execute tasks in parallel, bypassing the limitations of the Global Interpreter Lock (GIL) in CPython. This makes it ideal for CPU-bound tasks that require intensive computation.

Key Features of Multiprocessing

True Parallelism: Each process runs in its own memory space, allowing multiple processes to execute simultaneously on multi-core CPUs.

Bypasses GIL: Unlike threading, multiprocessing avoids the GIL, enabling efficient utilization of all available CPU cores.

Separate Memory: Processes do not share memory by default, reducing the risk of race conditions and making synchronization easier.

Applications of Multiprocessing

CPU-Bound Tasks: Suitable for tasks like image processing, scientific simulations, and numerical computations.

Data Processing Pipelines: Ideal for parallelizing tasks like data transformation and analysis.

Machine Learning: Often used for parallel data preprocessing or distributed training.

Example: Using Python's multiprocessing Module

python
Copy code

```
from multiprocessing import Process
import time
```

```python
def compute_task(name):
    print(f"Task {name} starting")
    time.sleep(2)  # Simulate computation
    print(f"Task {name} completed")

if __name__ == "__main__":
    processes = []
    for i in range(4):
        process = Process(target=compute_task, args=(i,))
        processes.append(process)
        process.start()

    for process in processes:
        process.join()

    print("All tasks completed.")
```

Benefits of Multiprocessing

Efficient for CPU-intensive tasks.

Fully utilizes multi-core processors.

Reduces contention caused by shared resources.

Challenges

Higher memory usage due to separate processes.
Increased complexity in inter-process communication
(IPC) compared to threads.
Overhead of process creation and management.

By using multiprocessing effectively, Python developers
can achieve significant performance improvements in
computationally intensive applications.

4.1. Introduction to the Multiprocessing Module

The multiprocessing module in Python is a powerful
library designed to enable parallel execution of tasks by
creating multiple processes. Unlike threading, which
runs multiple threads in the same process, the
multiprocessing module allows for the creation of

independent processes, each with its own memory space. This enables Python programs to fully utilize multi-core processors, bypassing the limitations of the Global Interpreter Lock (GIL) in CPython.

The module provides an easy-to-use interface for spawning and managing processes, making it suitable for both CPU-bound tasks and applications requiring true parallelism.

Key Features of the Multiprocessing Module

Process-Based Parallelism: Each process operates independently with its own memory, avoiding the bottlenecks caused by shared resources in threading.
Full CPU Utilization: By leveraging multiple cores, the module ensures that CPU-bound tasks run efficiently.
Built-In Synchronization Tools: Provides tools like locks, queues, and pipes to facilitate inter-process communication and synchronization.
Simple API: Offers a high-level interface similar to the threading module, making it easy for developers to use.

Common Components of the

Multiprocessing Module

Process: Represents an individual process that can execute a target function.

Example:

python
Copy code
```python
from multiprocessing import Process

def task():
    print("Hello from a new process!")

if __name__ == "__main__":
    p = Process(target=task)
    p.start()
    p.join()
```

Queue: A thread-safe data structure for communication between processes.

Example:

```python
Copy code
from multiprocessing import Process, Queue

def producer(queue):
    queue.put("Data from producer")

def consumer(queue):
    print(queue.get())

if __name__ == "__main__":
    q = Queue()
    p1 = Process(target=producer, args=(q,))
    p2 = Process(target=consumer, args=(q,))
    p1.start()
    p2.start()
    p1.join()
    p2.join()
```

Pool: Manages a pool of worker processes for parallel execution of tasks.

Example:
python
Copy code
from multiprocessing import Pool

```python
def square(n):
    return n * n

if __name__ == "__main__":
    with Pool(4) as pool:
        results = pool.map(square, [1, 2, 3, 4])
        print(results)  # Output: [1, 4, 9, 16]
```

Lock: Prevents race conditions by ensuring only one process accesses a resource at a time.

Benefits of the Multiprocessing Module

True Parallelism: Unlike threading, which is constrained by the GIL, multiprocessing allows multiple processes to execute simultaneously, utilizing multiple CPU cores.

Isolation: Each process has its own memory space, reducing the risks of data corruption and race conditions.

Scalability: Ideal for scaling CPU-bound tasks across multi-core systems.

Use Cases

CPU-Intensive Tasks: Suitable for applications like image processing, numerical simulations, and scientific computing.

Data Pipelines: Efficient for processing large datasets in parallel.

Web Scraping: Distributes scraping tasks across multiple processes to handle large-scale data extraction.

The multiprocessing module is an essential tool for Python developers aiming to write high-performance applications that leverage the full capabilities of modern multi-core processors. Its straightforward interface and robust features make it a preferred choice for parallel and distributed computing tasks.

4.2. Creating Processes in Python

In Python, creating processes is made straightforward by the multiprocessing module, which provides the Process class to create and manage individual processes. A process is an independent unit of execution that runs its own instance of the Python interpreter and has its own memory space. This is particularly useful for parallelizing tasks and fully utilizing multi-core CPUs.

The Process Class
The Process class is the foundation of the multiprocessing module. It represents a single process

and provides methods to start, run, and terminate the process.

Steps to Create a Process

Import the Process Class: Start by importing Process from the multiprocessing module.
Define a Target Function: This function contains the code that the process will execute.
Create a Process Object: Instantiate the Process class, specifying the target function and any arguments.
Start the Process: Use the start() method to begin execution.
Wait for Completion: Use the join() method to wait for the process to finish.

Example: Creating and Running a Process
python
Copy code

```python
from multiprocessing import Process

def task(name):
    print(f"Hello, {name} from a new process!")
```

```python
if __name__ == "__main__":
    # Create a process
    process = Process(target=task, args=("Python Developer",))

    # Start the process
    process.start()

    # Wait for the process to complete
    process.join()

    print("Process completed.")
```
Output:

arduino

Copy code

Hello, Python Developer from a new process!

Process completed.

Attributes and Methods of the Process Class

start(): Starts the execution of the process.

join(): Blocks the main process until the child process finishes.

is_alive(): Checks if the process is still running.

terminate(): Stops the process forcefully.

pid: Returns the process ID.

Example: Creating Multiple Processes
python
Copy code

```python
from multiprocessing import Process

def print_numbers(start, end):
    for i in range(start, end):
        print(i, end=" ")

if __name__ == "__main__":
    processes = []

    # Create and start multiple processes
    for i in range(5):
        p = Process(target=print_numbers, args=(i * 10, (i + 1) * 10))
        processes.append(p)
```

```
p.start()

# Wait for all processes to complete
for p in processes:
    p.join()

print("\nAll processes completed.")
```

Benefits of Using Processes

True Parallelism: Processes run on separate cores, enabling CPU-bound tasks to execute faster.
Memory Isolation: Each process has its own memory space, reducing interference between tasks.
Avoiding the GIL: Processes are unaffected by the Global Interpreter Lock, unlike threads.

Challenges

Overhead: Creating and managing processes involves more overhead compared to threads.

Inter-Process Communication: Processes don't share memory, so communication requires additional mechanisms like queues or pipes.

Resource Usage: Processes consume more memory compared to threads since each process has its own memory space.

Conclusion

Creating processes in Python using the multiprocessing module is an effective way to achieve concurrency and parallelism. By carefully designing processes and managing resources, developers can build high-performance applications that leverage the full power of multi-core CPUs.

4.3. Process Pools and Shared Memory

The multiprocessing module in Python provides powerful tools for creating and managing processes. Among these tools, Process Pools and Shared Memory play key roles in optimizing parallel execution and enabling inter-process communication.

Process Pools

A Process Pool is a collection of worker processes that can execute tasks in parallel. Instead of manually creating and managing individual processes, you can use a pool to distribute tasks among a predefined number of worker processes. This is particularly useful for tasks that are independent and can run concurrently.

Key Features:

Simplifies the management of multiple processes.
Reuses worker processes for multiple tasks, reducing overhead.
Provides high-level methods like map(), apply(), and starmap() for task distribution.

Example: Using a Process Pool

python

Copy code

```python
from multiprocessing import Pool

def square(number):
    return number * number

if __name__ == "__main__":
    with Pool(4) as pool:   # Create a pool with 4 worker processes
        numbers = [1, 2, 3, 4, 5]
        results = pool.map(square, numbers)
        print("Squared numbers:", results)
```

Output:

less

Copy code

```
Squared numbers: [1, 4, 9, 16, 25]
```

Methods in Process Pools:

map(func, iterable): Applies func to each item in the iterable and collects the results.

apply(func, args): Applies func to the specified arguments (synchronous).

apply_async(func, args): Asynchronously applies func to the specified arguments.

starmap(func, iterable): Similar to map, but supports multiple arguments for func.

Shared Memory

In multiprocessing, each process has its own memory space. However, there are scenarios where processes need to share data efficiently. The multiprocessing.shared_memory module allows processes to share data without creating duplicates, improving performance and reducing memory usage.

Key Features:

Facilitates efficient inter-process communication.
Avoids the overhead of serializing and copying data between processes.
Ideal for large datasets like arrays or matrices.

Example: Using Shared Memory

```python
Copy code
from multiprocessing import shared_memory
import numpy as np

# Create a shared memory block
shared_data = shared_memory.SharedMemory(create=True, size=100)

# Write data to shared memory
array = np.ndarray((10,), dtype=np.int64, buffer=shared_data.buf)
array[:] = np.arange(10)  # Fill the array with values

# Access the shared memory in a new process
print("Shared Memory Content:", array[:])

# Close and unlink the shared memory
shared_data.close()
shared_data.unlink()
```

Output:

css
Copy code
Shared Memory Content: [0 1 2 3 4 5 6 7 8 9]

When to Use Shared Memory:

Large Data Sharing: Efficient for large datasets like matrices or images.
Read/Write Access: When multiple processes need read/write access to shared data.

Challenges:

Requires careful synchronization to avoid data corruption (e.g., using locks).
Managing shared memory lifecycle (e.g., closing and unlinking) is essential to prevent memory leaks.

.

Combining Process Pools and Shared Memory

Process pools and shared memory can be used together to achieve both parallel task execution and efficient data sharing.

Example: Shared Memory with Process Pool

```python
Copy code
from multiprocessing import Pool, shared_memory
import numpy as np

def process_task(index):
    # Attach to existing shared memory
    existing_shm = shared_memory.SharedMemory(name="shared_array")
    array = np.ndarray((10,), dtype=np.int64, buffer=existing_shm.buf)
    return array[index] ** 2  # Return the square of the value at the given index

if __name__ == "__main__":
    # Create shared memory and write data
    shm = shared_memory.SharedMemory(create=True, size=100)
    array = np.ndarray((10,), dtype=np.int64, buffer=shm.buf)
```

```python
array[:] = np.arange(10)

# Use a process pool to perform tasks
with Pool(4) as pool:
    results = pool.map(process_task, range(10))

print("Processed Results:", results)

# Clean up shared memory
shm.close()
shm.unlink()
```

Output:

less

Copy code

Processed Results: [0, 1, 4, 9, 16, 25, 36, 49, 64, 81]

Benefits of Process Pools and Shared Memory

Efficiency: Process pools optimize resource utilization by reusing processes, and shared memory avoids data duplication.

Scalability: Enables the handling of large datasets and computationally intensive tasks across multiple cores.

Flexibility: Combines parallel task execution with efficient inter-process communication.

Challenges

Synchronization: Shared memory requires careful synchronization to avoid race conditions.
Resource Management: Proper cleanup of shared memory and process pools is necessary to prevent resource leaks.
Complexity: Combining shared memory with process pools adds complexity to program design.

Conclusion

Process pools and shared memory are essential components of the multiprocessing module, offering robust solutions for parallel execution and efficient data sharing. Together, they enable developers to write high-performance, scalable applications that fully utilize modern multi-core processors while managing memory effectively.

4.4. Inter-process Communication

Inter-Process Communication (IPC) is the mechanism by which processes exchange data or messages in a multiprocessing environment. Since processes have separate memory spaces, they cannot share data directly like threads. Python's multiprocessing module provides various tools to facilitate communication between processes, such as queues, pipes, and shared memory.

Why is IPC Necessary?

Data Sharing: Processes need a way to share results or inputs without duplicating memory.

Coordination: Processes may need to synchronize tasks or exchange signals to avoid conflicts or race conditions.

Efficiency: IPC mechanisms allow for streamlined data transfer without requiring external storage like files.

IPC Mechanisms in Python

1. Queues

A queue is a thread- and process-safe data structure provided by the multiprocessing module. It allows processes to exchange data in a first-in-first-out (FIFO) manner.

Example: Using a Queue for IPC
python
Copy code

```python
from multiprocessing import Process, Queue

def producer(queue):
    for i in range(5):
        queue.put(i)
        print(f"Produced: {i}")

def consumer(queue):
```

```python
    while not queue.empty():
        item = queue.get()
        print(f"Consumed: {item}")

if __name__ == "__main__":
    queue = Queue()
    p1 = Process(target=producer, args=(queue,))
    p2 = Process(target=consumer, args=(queue,))

    p1.start()
    p1.join()  # Wait for producer to finish

    p2.start()
    p2.join()  # Wait for consumer to finish
```

Output:

makefile

Copy code

Produced: 0

Produced: 1

Produced: 2

Produced: 3

Produced: 4

Consumed: 0

Consumed: 1

Consumed: 2

Consumed: 3

Consumed: 4

2. Pipes

A pipe provides a direct channel for two processes to communicate. It supports duplex (two-way) or half-duplex (one-way) communication.

Example: Using a Pipe for IPC
python
Copy code
```python
from multiprocessing import Process, Pipe

def sender(conn):
    conn.send("Hello from sender!")
    conn.close()

def receiver(conn):
    message = conn.recv()
    print(f"Received: {message}")
```

```python
if __name__ == "__main__":
    parent_conn, child_conn = Pipe()
    p1 = Process(target=sender, args=(child_conn,))
    p2 = Process(target=receiver, args=(parent_conn,))

    p1.start()
    p2.start()

    p1.join()
    p2.join()
```
Output:

vbnet

Copy code

Received: Hello from sender!

3. Shared Memory

Shared memory allows processes to share data directly without copying it. Python's multiprocessing.shared_memory module provides tools to create and manage shared memory blocks.

Example: Using Shared Memory

python

Copy code

```python
from multiprocessing import Process, shared_memory
import numpy as np

def worker(name):
    existing_shm = shared_memory.SharedMemory(name=name)
    data = np.ndarray((5,), dtype=np.int64, buffer=existing_shm.buf)
    data[0] += 1  # Modify shared data
    existing_shm.close()

if __name__ == "__main__":
    shm = shared_memory.SharedMemory(create=True, size=40)
    data = np.ndarray((5,), dtype=np.int64, buffer=shm.buf)
    data[:] = np.arange(5)

    p = Process(target=worker, args=(shm.name,))
    p.start()
```

```
p.join()

print("Modified Shared Data:", data[:])
shm.close()
shm.unlink()
```

Output:
less
Copy code
Modified Shared Data: [1 1 2 3 4]

Synchronization Tools for IPC

To prevent race conditions when multiple processes access shared data, synchronization tools such as locks and semaphores are used.

Example: Using a Lock
python
Copy code
```
from multiprocessing import Process, Lock

def task(lock, name):
```

```python
    with lock:
        print(f"{name} is accessing shared resource")

if __name__ == "__main__":
    lock = Lock()
    processes = [Process(target=task, args=(lock, f"Process
{i}")) for i in range(3)]

    for p in processes:
        p.start()
    for p in processes:
        p.join()
```

Output:

vbnet

Copy code

Process 0 is accessing shared resource

Process 1 is accessing shared resource

Process 2 is accessing shared resource

Choosing the Right IPC Mechanism

Mechanism	Use Case
Queue	Task queues or producer-consumer patterns.
Pipe	Simple, low-overhead communication between two processes.
Shared Memory	High-performance data sharing for large datasets.

Challenges of IPC

Synchronization: Proper use of locks and semaphores is essential to avoid race conditions.

Complexity: IPC adds complexity to program design.
Performance Overhead: Some IPC mechanisms (e.g., queues) may introduce latency.

Conclusion

Inter-process communication is essential for building efficient, parallel applications in Python. With tools like queues, pipes, and shared memory, Python's multiprocessing module provides robust mechanisms to facilitate data exchange and synchronization between processes. By choosing the appropriate IPC method for your use case, you can achieve high-performance, scalable applications.

4.5. Scaling Python Applications with Multiprocessing

When building Python applications, scaling becomes a critical factor, especially when dealing with CPU-bound tasks. Python's Global Interpreter Lock (GIL) can limit the ability to efficiently utilize multiple CPU cores in multi-threaded applications. This is where the multiprocessing module comes into play, enabling true parallel execution by leveraging multiple processes.

What is Multiprocessing in Python?

The multiprocessing module in Python allows you to create and manage multiple processes, enabling parallel execution of tasks. Unlike threading, which operates within a single process and is bound by the GIL, multiprocessing spawns separate processes, each with its own Python interpreter and memory space. This makes it ideal for CPU-bound operations such as numerical computations or data processing.

Key Features of Multiprocessing

Process-Based Parallelism: Each process runs independently, with its own memory space, avoiding the limitations of the GIL.

Shared Data Handling: It supports sharing data between processes using shared memory or message-passing mechanisms like Queue and Pipe.

Easy API: The interface of multiprocessing is similar to the threading module, making it intuitive for developers already familiar with threading.

Basic Example

```python
Copy code
import multiprocessing

def worker_function(number):
    print(f"Processing {number}")

if __name__ == "__main__":
    processes = []
    for i in range(5):
        process = multiprocessing.Process(target=worker_function, args=(i,))
```

```python
        processes.append(process)
        process.start()

    for process in processes:
        process.join()
```

This example creates five separate processes, each executing the worker_function.

Common Patterns in Multiprocessing

1. Using a Pool of Workers

The Pool class provides a convenient way to parallelize execution across a pool of worker processes.

python
Copy code
```python
from multiprocessing import Pool

def square(number):
    return number * number
```

```python
if __name__ == "__main__":
    numbers = [1, 2, 3, 4, 5]
    with Pool(processes=3) as pool:
        results = pool.map(square, numbers)
    print(results)  # Output: [1, 4, 9, 16, 25]
```

2. Interprocess Communication

Use Queue or Pipe for passing messages between processes.

python
Copy code
```python
from multiprocessing import Process, Queue

def producer(queue):
    queue.put("Hello from producer!")

def consumer(queue):
    print(queue.get())

if __name__ == "__main__":
    q = Queue()
```

```
p1 = Process(target=producer, args=(q,))
p2 = Process(target=consumer, args=(q,))
p1.start()
p2.start()
p1.join()
p2.join()
```

Advantages of Multiprocessing

True Parallelism: Fully utilizes multiple CPU cores.
Bypassing GIL: Overcomes the limitations of Python's threading.
Scalability: Suitable for CPU-intensive tasks like data analysis, image processing, and scientific computations.

Challenges and Considerations

Overhead: Spawning processes involves overhead compared to threading.
Memory Usage: Each process has its own memory space, which can lead to higher memory consumption.

Complex Debugging: Debugging multiprocessing code can be more challenging due to separate process contexts.

Serialization: Data passed between processes must be serializable using pickle.

Conclusion

Python's multiprocessing module is a powerful tool for scaling applications, particularly for CPU-bound tasks. By leveraging separate processes, it enables efficient utilization of modern multi-core processors. However, developers must carefully manage interprocess communication and resource overhead to build scalable and performant applications.

Chapter 5

Asynchronous Programming with asyncio

The asyncio module in Python facilitates asynchronous programming, allowing programs to handle multiple tasks concurrently without blocking the main thread. It is especially useful for I/O-bound tasks such as network requests, file operations, or database queries.

Key components of asyncio:

1. Event Loop: Manages and schedules asynchronous tasks.

2. Coroutines: Functions defined with async def, which can pause execution with await.

3. Tasks: Higher-level constructs that run coroutines concurrently.

4. Futures: Represent eventual results of asynchronous operations

Example of asyncio:

```python
import asyncio

async def async_task():
    print("Task started...")
    await asyncio.sleep(2)  # Non-blocking delay
    print("Task completed!")

async def main():
    await asyncio.gather(async_task(), async_task())  # Run tasks concurrently

asyncio.run(main())
```

This code demonstrates how asyncio executes tasks concurrently, making better use of system resources for tasks that involve waiting or delays.

5.1. What is Asynchronous Programming?

Asynchronous Programming is a programming paradigm that allows tasks to execute independently of the main program flow, enabling a system to handle multiple operations concurrently without waiting for one task to complete before starting another. This approach is especially effective for tasks that involve I/O operations, such as network requests, file handling, or database queries.

Key Features of Asynchronous Programming:

1. Non-blocking Execution: Tasks that involve waiting (e.g., for user input or data retrieval) do not block the execution of other tasks.

2. Concurrency: Multiple operations can run "at the same time" without necessarily running in parallel on multiple CPU cores.

3. Efficiency: Resources are used more effectively, reducing idle time and increasing responsiveness.

How It Works:

Asynchronous programming uses constructs like callbacks, promises, or async/await to manage operations that take time to complete. In Python, asyncio is a popular framework for implementing asynchronous code.

Example (Python):

```python
import asyncio

async def fetch_data():
    print("Fetching data...")
    await asyncio.sleep(2)  # Simulates a time-consuming task
    print("Data fetched!")
```

```
async def main():
    await asyncio.gather(fetch_data(), fetch_data())  # Run
tasks concurrently

asyncio.run(main())
```

This example shows how asynchronous programming allows multiple tasks to run concurrently, improving efficiency without blocking execution.

5.2. The asyncio Module: An Overview

The asyncio module in Python provides a framework for writing asynchronous programs. It is designed to handle I/O-bound tasks and high-level structured network code by enabling concurrency using coroutines, event loops, and non-blocking I/O operations.

Key Features of asyncio:

1. Event Loop: The core of asyncio, responsible for managing and scheduling asynchronous tasks.

2. Coroutines: Functions defined with async def that can pause and resume execution using await.

3. Tasks: Wrappers for coroutines that are scheduled and managed by the event loop for concurrent execution.

4. Futures: Represent a value that may become available at a later time.

5. Protocols and Transports: Support for implementing custom network communication protocols.

Benefits of Using asyncio:

Concurrency Without Threads: Achieves concurrency through cooperative multitasking, reducing the overhead of traditional threading.

Efficient Resource Usage: Suitable for tasks that spend time waiting for I/O operations, such as API requests or database queries.

Simplified Syntax: The async and await keywords make asynchronous code easier to write and understand.

Example:
```
import asyncio
async def task(name, delay):
    print(f"{name} started")
    await asyncio.sleep(delay)
    print(f"{name} finished")

async def main():
    await asyncio.gather(
        task("Task 1", 2),
        task("Task 2", 1),
    )

asyncio.run(main())
```

Use Cases:

Web scraping
Concurrent API requests
Real-time data processing

Network services (e.g., web servers or chat applications)

The asyncio module provides an effective way to manage asynchronous programming in Python, enhancing performance and responsiveness for modern applications.

5.3. Working with Coroutines

Coroutines are a fundamental concept in Python for asynchronous programming, allowing developers to write non-blocking code that executes efficiently, especially for I/O-bound tasks. They are a key feature of the asyncio library, enabling better resource management and responsiveness in applications.

What Are Coroutines?

A coroutine is a special type of function that can pause its execution (await) and resume later.
They are defined using the async def keyword and use the await keyword to yield control back to the event loop.

Example:

python
Copy code
import asyncio

```python
async def greet():
    print("Hello")
    await asyncio.sleep(1)  # Simulate an I/O operation
    print("World!")

# Running the coroutine
```

```
asyncio.run(greet())
```
Output:

```csharp
Copy code
Hello
[1 second pause]
World!
```

Key Features of Coroutines

Asynchronous Execution: They don't block the main thread while waiting for tasks like I/O operations.

Event Loop Management: Coroutines are executed within an event loop, which manages when they run and pause.

Non-blocking await: The await keyword allows waiting for asynchronous operations without halting the entire program.

Creating Coroutines

Use async def to define a coroutine.

Coroutines return a coroutine object, which must be awaited or scheduled in an event loop.

Example:

python
Copy code
```python
async def fetch_data():
    print("Fetching data...")
    await asyncio.sleep(2)
    return {"data": "sample"}
```

Running Coroutines

There are multiple ways to execute a coroutine:

Using asyncio.run():

python
Copy code

```python
result = asyncio.run(fetch_data())
print(result)
```

Scheduling Coroutines with

asyncio.create_task():

Allows multiple coroutines to run concurrently.
python
Copy code
```python
async def main():
    task = asyncio.create_task(fetch_data())
    print("Task scheduled...")
    data = await task
    print(data)

asyncio.run(main())
```

Using await in Nested Coroutines:

Coroutines can call and await other coroutines.
python
Copy code

```python
async def main():
    data = await fetch_data()
    print(data)

asyncio.run(main())
```

Concurrency with Coroutines

Coroutines can execute concurrently using asyncio.gather or asyncio.create_task. This is particularly useful for handling multiple I/O-bound tasks simultaneously.

Example:

python
Copy code
```python
async def download_file(file_id):
    print(f"Downloading file {file_id}...")
    await asyncio.sleep(2)
    print(f"File {file_id} downloaded.")
    return f"File {file_id}"
```

```python
async def main():
    results = await asyncio.gather(
        download_file(1),
        download_file(2),
        download_file(3)
    )
    print(results)

asyncio.run(main())
```
Output:

arduino
Copy code
Downloading file 1...
Downloading file 2...
Downloading file 3...
File 1 downloaded.
File 2 downloaded.
File 3 downloaded.
['File 1', 'File 2', 'File 3']

Error Handling in Coroutines

Use try...except blocks within coroutines to handle exceptions.

Example:

python
Copy code
```python
async def faulty_task():
    raise ValueError("Something went wrong!")

async def main():
    try:
        await faulty_task()
    except ValueError as e:
        print(f"Caught an error: {e}")

asyncio.run(main())
```
Output:

go
Copy code
```
Caught an error: Something went wrong!
```

Benefits of Coroutines

Efficiency: Ideal for I/O-bound tasks like database queries or API calls.

Concurrency: Allows multiple operations to progress without blocking.

Resource Management: Reduces the overhead of creating threads or processes.

Common Use Cases

Web Scraping: Making multiple HTTP requests concurrently.

Database Operations: Running queries without blocking the main application.

Real-Time Systems: Building responsive systems like chat applications.

Microservices: Handling asynchronous API calls between services.

Coroutines are a powerful tool for achieving asynchronous programming in Python, enabling efficient and scalable solutions for modern applications.

5.4. Event Loops and Task Scheduling

An event loop is the core mechanism in asynchronous programming that continuously checks for and executes tasks that are ready to run. It manages the scheduling of asynchronous tasks, ensuring they are executed in the right order without blocking the main thread.

Python's asyncio library provides a robust framework for event loop management and task scheduling, making it easier to write asynchronous and concurrent code.

What is an Event Loop?

The event loop is a system that runs in a single thread and coordinates the execution of multiple asynchronous tasks.

It works by repeatedly:

Checking for completed I/O operations or tasks ready to resume.

Scheduling their execution.

Continuing to the next ready task.

Example of an Event Loop in Python:

python
Copy code
```python
import asyncio

async def say_hello():
    print("Hello")
    await asyncio.sleep(1)  # Simulates a non-blocking I/O operation
    print("World!")

asyncio.run(say_hello())
```

Here, asyncio.run() initializes the event loop, which handles the coroutine say_hello().

Key Functions of the Event Loop

Run Tasks:

Executes coroutines or tasks asynchronously.

Schedule Tasks:

Schedules tasks (like I/O operations or coroutines) to be executed when their conditions are met.

Manage Timeouts:

Allows setting timers for tasks to execute after a specific delay.

Handle Callbacks:

Executes callbacks (functions triggered after a task completes) in the correct order.

Task Scheduling

In asyncio, tasks represent units of work that can be scheduled and executed concurrently.

Creating and Scheduling Tasks

Tasks are created using asyncio.create_task() or loop.create_task().

Example:

```python
Copy code
import asyncio

async def greet(name):
    await asyncio.sleep(1)
    print(f"Hello, {name}")

async def main():
    task1 = asyncio.create_task(greet("Alice"))
    task2 = asyncio.create_task(greet("Bob"))

    # Both tasks run concurrently
```

```
    await task1
    await task2

asyncio.run(main())
```
Output:

```
Copy code
Hello, Alice
Hello, Bob
```
Here, the tasks are executed concurrently using the event loop.

Running Multiple Tasks

asyncio provides utilities for running multiple tasks at the same time:

asyncio.gather:

Runs multiple coroutines concurrently and waits for all to complete.

Returns results as a list.

Example:

```python
Copy code
async def fetch_data(id):
    await asyncio.sleep(1)
    return f"Data {id}"


async def main():
    results = await asyncio.gather(fetch_data(1), fetch_data(2), fetch_data(3))
    print(results)


asyncio.run(main())
```

Output:

```css
Copy code
['Data 1', 'Data 2', 'Data 3']
asyncio.wait:
```

Runs multiple tasks but provides more control over their completion status.

Returns completed and pending tasks.

Timeouts with the Event Loop

You can set timeouts for tasks using asyncio.wait_for or asyncio.Timeout.

Example:

```python
Copy code
async def slow_task():
    await asyncio.sleep(5)

async def main():
    try:
        await asyncio.wait_for(slow_task(), timeout=2)
    except asyncio.TimeoutError:
        print("Task timed out!")
```

```
asyncio.run(main())
```

Output:

arduino
Copy code
Task timed out!

Using Callbacks

Callbacks are functions that run after a task completes.

Example:

python
Copy code
```
import asyncio

def on_complete(task):
    print(f"Task result: {task.result()}")

async def compute():
    return 42
```

```python
async def main():
    task = asyncio.create_task(compute())
    task.add_done_callback(on_complete)
    await task


asyncio.run(main())
```
Output:

```arduino
Copy code
Task result: 42
```

Best Practices for Event Loops and Tasks

Avoid Blocking Operations:

Don't use blocking I/O or sleep calls (time.sleep) within an asynchronous application.
Use non-blocking alternatives like asyncio.sleep.

Limit Task Count:

Avoid creating too many tasks, which can overwhelm the event loop and degrade performance.
Handle Exceptions Gracefully:

Always catch and handle exceptions within tasks to prevent crashes.

Run One Event Loop:

Only one event loop should run per thread; multiple loops in the same thread can cause conflicts.

Use Context Managers:

Use asyncio.run() for managing event loops instead of creating and managing loops manually.

Event Loop Example
Custom Event Loop Management:

```python
Copy code
import asyncio
```

```python
async def task_1():
    await asyncio.sleep(1)
    print("Task 1 complete")

async def task_2():
    await asyncio.sleep(2)
    print("Task 2 complete")

loop = asyncio.get_event_loop()
loop.run_until_complete(asyncio.gather(task_1(),
task_2()))
loop.close()
```

Conclusion

The event loop is the backbone of Python's asynchronous programming, enabling efficient execution of multiple tasks without blocking. Understanding event loop behavior and task scheduling mechanisms is crucial for building scalable and responsive applications.

5.5. Combining asyncio with Threading and Multiprocessing

In Python, asynchronous programming (asyncio), threading, and multiprocessing are complementary tools for achieving concurrency and parallelism. While asyncio is ideal for I/O-bound tasks, threading and multiprocessing excel in handling CPU-bound tasks or tasks requiring concurrent execution in separate threads or processes. Combining these approaches can enhance the performance and scalability of your application.

Key Concepts

asyncio:

Works within a single thread using an event loop.
Best for I/O-bound tasks (e.g., file operations, HTTP requests).

Threading:

Uses lightweight threads within a process.

Suitable for I/O-bound tasks that involve blocking operations.

Limited by the Global Interpreter Lock (GIL) for CPU-bound tasks.

Multiprocessing:

Spawns separate processes with independent memory.

Ideal for CPU-bound tasks as it bypasses the GIL.

Why Combine Them?

To handle blocking I/O tasks (e.g., file operations or legacy libraries) within asyncio.

To offload CPU-intensive tasks to separate processes.

To integrate with existing codebases using threading or multiprocessing.

Combining asyncio and Threading

You can run blocking code in separate threads without freezing the event loop using asyncio.to_thread. This allows asynchronous tasks to continue executing while the thread performs its work.

Example: Using asyncio.to_thread
python
Copy code

```python
import asyncio
import time

def blocking_task():
    time.sleep(2)  # Simulates a blocking I/O task
    return "Done"

async def main():
    print("Starting blocking task...")
    result = await asyncio.to_thread(blocking_task)
    print(result)

asyncio.run(main())
```

Output:

Copy code

Starting blocking task...

Done

Example: Using concurrent.futures.ThreadPoolExecutor
ThreadPoolExecutor can run tasks in a thread pool, integrated with asyncio.

```python
Copy code
import asyncio
from concurrent.futures import ThreadPoolExecutor

def blocking_task():
    return sum(range(1000000))

async def main():
    loop = asyncio.get_running_loop()
    with ThreadPoolExecutor() as pool:
        result = await loop.run_in_executor(pool, blocking_task)
    print(f"Result: {result}")

asyncio.run(main())
```

Combining asyncio and Multiprocessing

For CPU-bound tasks, you can use asyncio with multiprocessing. The asyncio event loop can work with ProcessPoolExecutor to execute tasks in separate processes.

Example: Using concurrent.futures.ProcessPoolExecutor

```python
Copy code
import asyncio
from concurrent.futures import ProcessPoolExecutor

def cpu_intensive_task(n):
    return sum(i * i for i in range(n))

async def main():
    loop = asyncio.get_running_loop()
    with ProcessPoolExecutor() as pool:
        result = await loop.run_in_executor(pool, cpu_intensive_task, 10**6)
```

```python
    print(f"Result: {result}")

asyncio.run(main())
```

Integrating All Three

In some cases, you might combine asyncio, threading, and multiprocessing in the same application. This is useful for systems with mixed workloads (e.g., I/O-bound tasks, CPU-bound tasks, and blocking operations).

Example: Combining All Approaches

```python
python
Copy code
import asyncio
import time
from concurrent.futures import

ThreadPoolExecutor, ProcessPoolExecutor

def blocking_task():
    time.sleep(2)  # Simulate blocking I/O
```

```python
    return "Blocking task complete"

def cpu_intensive_task(n):
    return sum(i * i for i in range(n))

async def async_task():
    await asyncio.sleep(1)
    print("Async task complete")

async def main():
    loop = asyncio.get_running_loop()

    # ThreadPoolExecutor for I/O-bound tasks
    with ThreadPoolExecutor() as thread_pool:
        blocking_result = await loop.run_in_executor(thread_pool, blocking_task)
        print(blocking_result)

    # ProcessPoolExecutor for CPU-bound tasks
    with ProcessPoolExecutor() as process_pool:
        cpu_result = await loop.run_in_executor(process_pool, cpu_intensive_task, 10**6)
```

```python
    print(f"CPU result: {cpu_result}")

    # Asyncio task
    await async_task()

asyncio.run(main())
```

Output:

```sql
Copy code
Blocking task complete
CPU result: 333332833333500000
Async task complete
```

Best Practices

Avoid Mixing Too Much:
Overusing threading and multiprocessing within asyncio can increase complexity and debugging challenges.

Use Appropriate Tools:

Use asyncio for I/O-bound tasks.

Use threading for lightweight blocking tasks.

Use multiprocessing for heavy CPU-bound tasks.

Graceful Shutdown:

Ensure proper cleanup of threads and processes.

Use asyncio context managers like with for executors.

When to Combine?

I/O-Heavy Applications: Use asyncio for network operations and threading for file I/O.

CPU-Intensive Workloads: Use multiprocessing to distribute tasks across multiple cores.

Legacy Code Integration: Wrap blocking code in threads or processes for non-blocking asyncio compatibility.

Combining these tools allows for flexible and scalable applications, leveraging the strengths of each concurrency model.

Chapter 6
Using Concurrent Futures for Simplicity

The concurrent.futures module in Python provides a high-level interface for asynchronously executing tasks using threads or processes. It is designed to simplify concurrent programming by abstracting away the complexities of managing threads and processes directly.

Key Features

ThreadPoolExecutor:

Executes tasks in a pool of threads.
Suitable for I/O-bound or lightweight tasks.

ProcessPoolExecutor:

Executes tasks in a pool of processes.

Ideal for CPU-bound tasks as it bypasses the Global Interpreter Lock (GIL).

Future Objects:

Represents the result of an asynchronous computation, which can be checked or retrieved later.

Why Use concurrent.futures?

Simplifies thread and process management.

Provides a consistent interface for both threading and multiprocessing.

Easily integrates with synchronous code.

Example: Using ThreadPoolExecutor
python
Copy code
```python
from concurrent.futures import ThreadPoolExecutor

def task(n):
```

```python
    return n * n

with ThreadPoolExecutor() as executor:
    results = list(executor.map(task, range(5)))
print(results)  # Output: [0, 1, 4, 9, 16]
```

Example: Using ProcessPoolExecutor
python
Copy code
```python
from concurrent.futures import ProcessPoolExecutor

def cpu_task(n):
    return sum(i * i for i in range(n))

with ProcessPoolExecutor() as executor:
    results = list(executor.map(cpu_task, [10**5, 10**6, 10**7]))
print(results)
```

Best Practices

Use ThreadPoolExecutor for I/O-bound tasks and ProcessPoolExecutor for CPU-bound tasks.

Use with to ensure proper cleanup of resources.

Use executor.submit() for finer control over individual tasks, or executor.map() for bulk operations.

concurrent.futures provides a simple, consistent way to handle concurrency, making it ideal for tasks that don't require the full complexity of asyncio.

6.1. Introduction to the concurrent.futures Module

The concurrent.futures module in Python provides a high-level interface for managing concurrency through threads and processes. It abstracts the complexities of threading and multiprocessing, offering a consistent and easy-to-use API for parallel task execution. Introduced in Python 3.2, the module is widely used for tasks such as I/O operations, computation-heavy processing, and asynchronous programming.

Core Components of concurrent.futures

Executor Classes:

ThreadPoolExecutor:

Executes tasks in a pool of threads.
Ideal for I/O-bound operations like file reading, network requests, and database queries.

ProcessPoolExecutor:

Executes tasks in a pool of processes.
Designed for CPU-intensive tasks as it avoids the Global Interpreter Lock (GIL).

Future Objects:

Represents the result of an asynchronous operation.
Provides methods like result() and done() to retrieve the result or check the task's status.

Why Use concurrent.futures?

Simplifies Concurrency:

Reduces the boilerplate code required for managing threads or processes.

Flexible Execution Models:

Choose between threads for lightweight tasks and processes for heavy computations.

Automatic Resource Management:

Executors handle resource allocation, queuing, and cleanup automatically.

Key Methods

submit(func, *args, **kwargs):

Submits a function to the executor for asynchronous execution.

Returns a Future object.

map(func, *iterables):

Applies a function to an iterable of arguments concurrently.
Returns an iterator of results.

shutdown(wait=True):

Gracefully shuts down the executor, waiting for all tasks to complete.

Example: ThreadPoolExecutor

python
Copy code
from concurrent.futures import ThreadPoolExecutor

def task(n):
    return n * n

with ThreadPoolExecutor(max_workers=3) as executor:
    futures = [executor.submit(task, i) for i in range(5)]
    results = [future.result() for future in futures]

print(results) # Output: [0, 1, 4, 9, 16]

Example: ProcessPoolExecutor
python
Copy code
```python
from concurrent.futures import ProcessPoolExecutor

def cpu_intensive_task(n):
    return sum(i * i for i in range(n))

with ProcessPoolExecutor(max_workers=2) as executor:
    results = list(executor.map(cpu_intensive_task, [10**5,
10**6, 10**7]))
print(results)
```

Advantages

Unified API:

Common interface for both threads and processes simplifies code.

Efficient Resource Use:

Executors manage the pool size and resource allocation efficiently.

Error Handling:

Futures allow capturing exceptions from tasks and handling them gracefully.

Use Cases

I/O-bound Tasks:

Downloading files, making API calls, or reading from a database.

CPU-bound Tasks:

Data processing, scientific simulations, and machine learning computations.

Parallelization:

Splitting large workloads into smaller tasks for concurrent execution.

The concurrent.futures module provides a simple and effective way to incorporate concurrency into Python applications, making it a valuable tool for developers aiming to improve performance and scalability.

6.2. ThreadPoolExecutor and ProcessPoolExecutor

The concurrent.futures module in Python provides two main classes for executing tasks concurrently: ThreadPoolExecutor and ProcessPoolExecutor. These classes simplify the management of threads and processes, enabling developers to execute tasks in parallel with minimal boilerplate code.

1. ThreadPoolExecutor

The ThreadPoolExecutor manages a pool of worker threads, making it ideal for executing I/O-bound or lightweight tasks that do not require heavy CPU processing.

Key Features

Executes tasks concurrently in threads within a single process.
Bypasses the overhead of process creation.
Affected by the Global Interpreter Lock (GIL), limiting its effectiveness for CPU-bound tasks.

Common Use Cases

I/O-bound tasks, such as reading/writing files or making HTTP requests.
Lightweight background operations.

Example: Using ThreadPoolExecutor
python
Copy code
from concurrent.futures import ThreadPoolExecutor

```python
def task(n):
    print(f"Task {n} running in thread")
    return n * n

with ThreadPoolExecutor(max_workers=3) as executor:
    futures = [executor.submit(task, i) for i in range(5)]
    results = [future.result() for future in futures]

print("Results:", results)
```

Output:

arduino
Copy code
Task 0 running in thread
Task 1 running in thread
Task 2 running in thread
Task 3 running in thread
Task 4 running in thread
Results: [0, 1, 4, 9, 16]

2. ProcessPoolExecutor

The ProcessPoolExecutor manages a pool of worker processes, making it suitable for executing CPU-bound tasks. Each task runs in a separate process, bypassing the GIL.

Key Features

Executes tasks in multiple processes, leveraging multiple CPU cores.
Each process has its own memory space, preventing shared memory conflicts.
Higher overhead compared to threads, due to process creation and communication.

Common Use Cases

CPU-bound tasks, such as mathematical computations or data processing.
Parallel execution of computationally intensive workloads.

Example: Using ProcessPoolExecutor
python

Copy code

```
from concurrent.futures import ProcessPoolExecutor

def cpu_intensive_task(n):
    return sum(i * i for i in range(n))

with ProcessPoolExecutor(max_workers=2) as executor:
    results = list(executor.map(cpu_intensive_task, [10**5,
10**6, 10**7]))

print("Results:", results)
```

Differences Between ThreadPoolExecutor and ProcessPoolExecutor

Feature	ThreadPoolExecutor	ProcessPoolExecutor
Concurrency Model	Threads (single process)	Processes (multiple processes)
Best For	I/O-bound tasks	CPU-bound

		tasks
Global Interpreter Lock(GIL)	Shared, limiting CPU-bound tasks	Not shared, suitable for parallel computation
Overhead	Low (threads are lightweight)	High (process creation overhead)
Memory	Shared between threads	Separate for each process

When to Use Each Executor

Use ThreadPoolExecutor for:

Making multiple HTTP requests concurrently.
Reading/writing large files without blocking.
Tasks where the bottleneck is I/O latency.

Use ProcessPoolExecutor for:

Performing data analysis or mathematical computations.
Image or video processing tasks.
Any workload that is computationally expensive and benefits from multiple CPU cores.

Advantages of Executors

Simplifies the creation and management of threads and processes.
Provides a unified interface for concurrency.
Ensures proper cleanup of resources with context managers (with).

Both ThreadPoolExecutor and ProcessPoolExecutor are powerful tools that make it easy to achieve concurrency in Python. Choosing the right one depends on the nature of the task—whether it is I/O-bound or CPU-bound.

6.3. Managing Futures and Results

In the concurrent.futures module, Future objects play a key role in managing and retrieving the results of asynchronous tasks. A Future represents the eventual result of an asynchronous computation and allows you to monitor and manage tasks that are running concurrently. Using ThreadPoolExecutor or ProcessPoolExecutor, you can submit tasks and get a Future object, which you can use to track their status, cancel them, and retrieve their results when they are done.

What is a Future?

A Future object encapsulates the result of an asynchronous operation that may not have completed yet. It provides methods for:

Checking if the task has completed.

Getting the result of the task once it is finished.

Handling exceptions raised by the task.

A Future can be obtained when submitting a task to an executor (via submit() or map()).

Key Methods of a Future Object

future.result():

Returns the result of the task when it completes.

If the task raised an exception, it will be re-raised.

python

Copy code

result = future.result() # Waits for the task to complete and returns its result

future.done():

Returns True if the task has finished executing, either successfully or with an exception.

python

Copy code

```
if future.done():
    print("Task is done")
```

```
future.cancel():
```

Attempts to cancel the execution of a task. Returns True if the task was successfully canceled, or False if it was already completed or cannot be canceled.

python

Copy code

```
if not future.done():
    future.cancel()
```

```
future.exception():
```

Returns the exception raised by the task, if any, or None if no exception occurred.

python

Copy code

```
exception = future.exception()
```

```
if exception:
```

```python
        print(f"Task failed with: {exception}")
```

```python
future.add_done_callback(fn):
```

Registers a callback function to be called when the task completes.

```python
python
Copy code
def callback(future):
    print(f"Task completed with result: {future.result()}")
```

```python
future.add_done_callback(callback)
```

Managing Multiple Futures

You often work with multiple tasks concurrently, so managing a collection of Future objects is essential. Here are ways to handle them efficiently:

Using as_completed():

Iterates over a set of futures as they complete, in the order they finish (not the order they were started).

python

Copy code

```python
from concurrent.futures import ThreadPoolExecutor

def task(n):
    return n * n

with ThreadPoolExecutor(max_workers=3) as executor:
    futures = [executor.submit(task, i) for i in range(5)]

    for future in concurrent.futures.as_completed(futures):
        print(f"Result: {future.result()}")
```

Output:

makefile

Copy code

```
Result: 0
Result: 1
Result: 4
Result: 9
Result: 16
```

Using wait():

Blocks until all the futures have finished executing. Returns two lists: the completed and the pending futures.

python
Copy code
```
from concurrent.futures import wait

with ThreadPoolExecutor(max_workers=3) as executor:
    futures = [executor.submit(task, i) for i in range(5)]

    completed, pending = wait(futures)
    for future in completed:
        print(f"Result: {future.result()}")
```

Handling Exceptions

When tasks submitted to the executor raise exceptions, they are captured by the Future object. You can check for exceptions by using the exception() method.

Example: Handling Exceptions

python
Copy code

```python
from concurrent.futures import ThreadPoolExecutor

def task(n):
    if n == 3:
        raise ValueError("An error occurred in task 3")
    return n * n

with ThreadPoolExecutor(max_workers=3) as executor:
    futures = [executor.submit(task, i) for i in range(5)]

    for future in futures:
        try:
            result = future.result()  # This will raise exceptions if any occurred
            print(f"Result: {result}")
        except Exception as e:
            print(f"Task failed with exception: {e}")
```

Output:

```vbnet
Copy code
Result: 0
Result: 1
Task failed with exception: An error occurred in task 3
Result: 9
Result: 16
```

Best Practices for Managing Futures

Always Handle Exceptions:

Use future.result() within a try-except block to gracefully handle task failures.

Use as_completed() for Better Control:

If you need to process results as tasks complete, use as_completed() instead of waiting for all tasks to finish.

Avoid Blocking:

Avoid blocking on result() calls when you can use other techniques like as_completed() or wait() to monitor multiple futures concurrently.

Leverage Callbacks:

For non-blocking tasks, use add_done_callback() to execute a function when a task finishes, allowing you to handle results or errors asynchronously.

Canceling Tasks:

Always check done() before attempting to cancel a task. If a task is already running or completed, it cannot be canceled.

Conclusion

Managing Future objects in Python's concurrent.futures module provides an easy and effective way to handle asynchronous tasks. With futures, you can:

Track the status of concurrent tasks.

Retrieve results once tasks are complete.

Handle exceptions that may arise during task execution. Using these tools, developers can write more efficient, scalable, and maintainable concurrent programs.

6.4. Best Practices for Using concurrent.futures

The concurrent.futures module provides an easy-to-use API for concurrent programming with threads and processes. While it abstracts away much of the complexity, there are still best practices to follow for optimal performance, readability, and maintainability when using ThreadPoolExecutor, ProcessPoolExecutor, and Future objects.

Here are some key best practices for using concurrent.futures effectively:

1. Choose the Right Executor

ThreadPoolExecutor: Best for I/O-bound tasks where operations like file I/O, network requests, or database access are the bottleneck. Threads are lightweight and share memory, making them suitable for tasks that are primarily waiting for external resources.

ProcessPoolExecutor: Best for CPU-bound tasks that require heavy computations (e.g., data processing, mathematical calculations). Processes run independently, each having its own memory space, making them more suitable for parallelizing tasks and bypassing the Global Interpreter Lock (GIL).

Tip: Use ThreadPoolExecutor for tasks that involve I/O, and ProcessPoolExecutor for CPU-intensive tasks.

2. Limit the Number of Workers

When creating an executor, it's important to manage the number of worker threads or processes effectively. Too many workers can overwhelm the system with context switching and lead to diminishing returns.

Threads: Typically, the optimal number of threads should be equal to the number of I/O operations you're trying to handle concurrently.

Processes: For CPU-bound tasks, the ideal number of processes is usually the number of CPU cores available on the machine.

Tip: Use max_workers wisely. For threads, a larger pool may not always be better. For processes, the number of workers should typically not exceed the number of available CPU cores.

3. Use Context Managers to Ensure Proper Cleanup

Always use executors within a with statement to ensure that resources are cleaned up properly after use. This guarantees that the executor is shut down, preventing resource leaks or incomplete task execution.

python
Copy code

```
from concurrent.futures import ThreadPoolExecutor

def task(n):
    return n * n

with ThreadPoolExecutor(max_workers=3) as executor:
    results = list(executor.map(task, range(5)))
print(results)
```

Using with handles the shutdown process automatically, ensuring that all threads or processes complete before the program exits.

4. Avoid Blocking on Tasks When Possible

Blocking calls like future.result() can halt the progress of your program. Instead, use as_completed() or wait() to manage multiple futures concurrently.

as_completed(): Useful when you want to process results as tasks finish, rather than waiting for all tasks to complete.

python

Copy code

```python
from concurrent.futures import ThreadPoolExecutor, as_completed

def task(n):
    return n * n

with ThreadPoolExecutor() as executor:
    futures = [executor.submit(task, i) for i in range(5)]
    for future in as_completed(futures):
        print(future.result())
```

wait(): If you want to block until all futures are done, wait() is useful, but it returns two lists (completed and pending), so you can check which tasks are finished.

python

Copy code

```python
from concurrent.futures import wait

with ThreadPoolExecutor() as executor:
    futures = [executor.submit(task, i) for i in range(5)]
    completed, pending = wait(futures)
```

```python
    for future in completed:
        print(future.result())
```

5. Handle Exceptions Properly

Tasks may fail due to various reasons (e.g., invalid input, timeouts). Always handle exceptions raised during task execution to prevent the program from crashing.

future.result(): If a task raises an exception, it will be re-raised when calling result(). Wrap calls to result() in a try-except block to handle exceptions gracefully.

python
Copy code
```python
def task(n):
    if n == 3:
        raise ValueError("Error in task 3")
    return n * n
```

with ThreadPoolExecutor() as executor:

```python
    futures = [executor.submit(task, i) for i in range(5)]
```

```python
for future in futures:
    try:
        result = future.result()  # Will raise the exception if any
        print(result)
    except Exception as e:
        print(f"Task failed with exception: {e}")
```

future.exception(): You can also check if a task failed by using the exception() method on a Future object.

python
Copy code

```python
if future.exception():
    print(f"Task failed with exception: {future.exception()}")
```

6. Use add_done_callback() for

Non-Blocking Completion Handling

If you want to process the result of a task as soon as it completes without blocking the main thread, you can use add_done_callback(). This allows you to attach a callback function that will be executed when the task finishes.

python
Copy code
```python
from concurrent.futures import ThreadPoolExecutor

def task(n):
    return n * n

def callback(future):
    print(f"Task completed with result: {future.result()}")

with ThreadPoolExecutor() as executor:

    future = executor.submit(task, 5)
    future.add_done_callback(callback)
```

This approach is useful when you need to perform some action as soon as a task finishes, without waiting for all tasks to complete.

7. Avoid Using map() for Blocking Tasks

While executor.map() can be convenient for applying a function to an iterable, it blocks until all tasks are finished, which may not be ideal for long-running or blocking operations. For non-blocking or concurrent execution of tasks, prefer using submit() or as_completed().

Tip: Use submit() for more control over individual tasks, and reserve map() for cases where you want to run a function on an iterable and collect results.

8. Limit Task Dependencies

Avoid tasks that depend on the results of other tasks in a way that would force you to block or wait unnecessarily. If tasks are dependent on each other, consider restructuring the tasks into smaller, independent units that can be processed concurrently.

9. Be Cautious with Shared Data

When working with ThreadPoolExecutor, multiple threads share the same memory space, which can lead to race conditions and data corruption. To mitigate this, use thread-safe data structures or synchronization primitives like threading.Lock or threading.Semaphore.

For ProcessPoolExecutor, each process has its own memory space, so shared data must be passed through inter-process communication (IPC) mechanisms like Queue or Pipe.

10. Monitor Task Progress

For long-running tasks, it's often helpful to monitor progress. You can do this by periodically checking the status of each Future object using done() or running().

python
Copy code
```python
def task(n):
    for i in range(n):
        if i % 1000 == 0:
            print(f"Progress: {i}")
```

```
    return n

with ThreadPoolExecutor() as executor:
    futures = [executor.submit(task, 10000) for _ in
range(3)]
    while futures:
        for future in futures:
            if future.done():
                print(f"Task result: {future.result()}")
                futures.remove(future)
```

Conclusion

Following these best practices can help you write efficient, maintainable, and bug-free concurrent code using concurrent.futures. Always:

Choose the appropriate executor for your task type.
Handle exceptions and manage task results properly.
Ensure proper resource cleanup using context managers.

Avoid blocking calls and leverage callbacks and as_completed() for greater flexibility.

By adhering to these practices, you can maximize the power of concurrent programming in Python, ensuring that your application is both scalable and robust.

Chapter 7
Parallel Algorithms and Patterns

Parallel algorithms are designed to divide a problem into smaller subproblems that can be solved concurrently, leveraging multiple processors or cores to enhance performance. They are essential for maximizing the efficiency of multicore systems and distributed computing environments. These algorithms often follow well-established patterns that simplify their design and implementation.

Common Parallel Patterns

Data Parallelism:

Splits data into independent chunks that can be processed concurrently.

Common in tasks like array processing, image manipulation, and matrix operations.

Example: Applying a function to every element of a large dataset.

Task Parallelism:

Decomposes a problem into distinct tasks that can execute in parallel.

Tasks may involve different computations or operate on different parts of the data.

Example: Concurrently downloading files from multiple URLs.

Pipeline Parallelism:

Breaks a process into stages, with each stage performing a specific operation.

Data flows through the pipeline, with different stages processing it concurrently.

Example: Video processing with stages for decoding, filtering, and encoding.

Divide and Conquer:

Divides a problem into smaller subproblems, solves them concurrently, and combines the results.

Suitable for recursive algorithms like merge sort or quick sort.

Example: Splitting a dataset for parallel search or sorting.

Map-Reduce:

A two-step pattern involving a map operation (applying a function to data chunks) followed by a reduce operation (aggregating results).

Widely used in distributed computing systems like Hadoop or Spark.

Example: Counting word frequencies in a large text corpus.

Fork-Join:

Tasks are forked into multiple parallel subtasks, and results are joined once all subtasks complete.

Example: Recursive computations like parallel Fibonacci calculation.

Parallel Programming Libraries in Python
Python provides several libraries for implementing

parallel algorithms:

concurrent.futures: Simplifies task execution with thread and process pools.
multiprocessing: Enables process-based parallelism for CPU-bound tasks.
asyncio: Manages asynchronous I/O-bound operations.
Dask and Ray: Designed for scalable, distributed computing.

Use Cases

Data Analysis: Parallelizing computations for large datasets.
Machine Learning: Training models on large data using multiple GPUs/CPUs.

Scientific Computing: Simulations, matrix computations, and numerical solvers.

Web Crawling: Fetching data from multiple websites simultaneously.

Parallel algorithms and patterns empower developers to create scalable and efficient solutions, making them critical for high-performance computing in modern applications.

7.1. Map-Reduce Pattern

The Map-Reduce pattern is a powerful programming model widely used for processing large datasets in parallel and distributed systems. It splits a problem into two phases—Map and Reduce—making it well-suited for tasks like data analysis, aggregation, and transformation. This pattern is foundational in systems like Hadoop, Apache Spark, and other big data platforms.

How It Works

Map Phase:

The input data is divided into smaller chunks.
Each chunk is processed independently by applying a map function, which transforms the data into key-value pairs.

Shuffle and Sort:

After mapping, the intermediate key-value pairs are grouped by keys.
This step ensures that all values corresponding to the same key are collected together.

Reduce Phase:

A reduce function is applied to the grouped data, aggregating or summarizing the values associated with each key.

The final result is a smaller, processed dataset.

Example

Word Count Using Map-Reduce

Problem: Count the frequency of words in a large text file.

Map Phase:

Split the text into words.

For each word, emit a key-value pair (word, 1).

Shuffle and Sort:

Group all key-value pairs by the word key, so [(word1, 1), (word1, 1)] becomes [(word1, [1, 1])].

Reduce Phase:

Sum the values for each key, resulting in [(word1, 2)].

Python Implementation:

```python
Copy code
from collections import defaultdict

# Sample data
text = "hello world hello map reduce map reduce"

# Map phase
def map_phase(data):
    for word in data.split():
        yield word, 1

# Shuffle and Sort
def shuffle_and_sort(mapped_data):
    grouped_data = defaultdict(list)
    for key, value in mapped_data:
        grouped_data[key].append(value)
    return grouped_data
```

```python
# Reduce phase
def reduce_phase(grouped_data):
    for key, values in grouped_data.items():
        yield key, sum(values)

# Map step
mapped = list(map_phase(text))

# Shuffle and Sort step
grouped = shuffle_and_sort(mapped)

# Reduce step
reduced = list(reduce_phase(grouped))

print(reduced)  # Output: [('hello', 2), ('world', 1), ('map', 2), ('reduce', 2)]
```

Applications

Big Data Processing:

Used in distributed systems like Hadoop and Spark to process petabytes of data.

Examples: Log analysis, indexing, and clickstream analysis.

Data Aggregation:

Summing, averaging, or finding maximum/minimum values in large datasets.

Data Transformation:

Converting or filtering large datasets.

Machine Learning:

Preparing data for training models or distributed computations.

Advantages

Scalability: Handles massive datasets across distributed systems.
Fault Tolerance: Intermediate data can be reprocessed if a node fails.

Simplicity: Easy to implement and parallelize for tasks involving large-scale data processing.

Disadvantages

High Latency: Due to disk-based intermediate data in traditional implementations like Hadoop.
Not Ideal for Iterative Algorithms: Requires repeated map-reduce steps for iterative tasks like machine learning.

The Map-Reduce pattern provides a simple yet robust framework for processing vast amounts of data in parallel. By splitting tasks into independent, reusable phases, it enables efficient distributed computing in modern data-driven applications.

7.2. Divide and Conquer

The Divide and Conquer paradigm is a powerful algorithm design technique that involves breaking a problem into smaller subproblems, solving these subproblems independently, and then combining their solutions to solve the original problem. This approach is particularly useful for solving problems that can be naturally divided into similar smaller parts.

Steps in Divide and Conquer

Divide:

Break the problem into smaller, independent subproblems.
These subproblems should ideally be of the same type as the original problem.

Conquer:

Solve each subproblem recursively. If the subproblem size is small enough, solve it directly (base case).

Combine:

Merge the solutions of the subproblems to form the solution to the original problem.

Key Characteristics

Recursion: Divide and Conquer algorithms are often implemented recursively.
Independence: Subproblems are solved independently, which allows for parallelism in some cases.
Merge Step: The results of subproblems are combined efficiently, often in linear time relative to the size of the data.

Examples of Divide and Conquer Algorithms

Merge Sort:

Divide: Split the array into two halves.
Conquer: Recursively sort each half.
Combine: Merge the two sorted halves into a single sorted array.

Time Complexity:

O

(

n

log

n

)

O(nlogn).

python
Copy code
```python
def merge_sort(arr):
    if len(arr) <= 1:
        return arr
    mid = len(arr) // 2
    left = merge_sort(arr[:mid])
    right = merge_sort(arr[mid:])
    return merge(left, right)

def merge(left, right):
    result = []
    i = j = 0
```

```
while i < len(left) and j < len(right):
    if left[i] < right[j]:
        result.append(left[i])
        i += 1
    else:
        result.append(right[j])
        j += 1
result.extend(left[i:])
result.extend(right[j:])
return result
```

Quick Sort:

Divide: Choose a pivot and partition the array into elements less than and greater than the pivot.
Conquer: Recursively sort the partitions.
Combine: The partitions are combined automatically as the recursion unwinds.

Time Complexity: Average

O

$($

n

$\log$

n

)

O(nlogn), Worst

O

(

n

2

)

O(n

2

).

Binary Search:

Divide: Split the search space into two halves.
Conquer: Recursively search the relevant half.
Combine: Return the result of the search.

Time Complexity:

O

(

log

n

)

O(logn).

Matrix Multiplication (Strassen's Algorithm):

Divide: Split the matrices into smaller submatrices.

Conquer: Perform recursive multiplications on the submatrices.

Combine: Merge the results to form the final matrix.

Closest Pair of Points:

Divide: Split the points into two halves.

Conquer: Find the closest pair in each half.

Combine: Check for the closest pair across the dividing line.

Applications

Sorting: Algorithms like Merge Sort and Quick Sort.

Searching: Binary Search in sorted arrays.

Dynamic Programming: Optimizing certain recursive problems by memoizing subproblem results.

Computational Geometry: Problems like closest pair of points and convex hull.

Parallel Computing: Breaking down problems into independent parts for distributed processing.

Advantages

Efficiency: Many divide-and-conquer algorithms, like Merge Sort, achieve better time complexity than iterative counterparts.

Parallelism: Subproblems can often be solved concurrently, enabling performance gains on multicore systems.

Modularity: Breaking a problem into smaller pieces makes the algorithm easier to design, implement, and debug.

Disadvantages

Overhead: Recursive calls and the combine step can introduce overhead.

Not Always Applicable: Some problems cannot be easily divided into independent subproblems.

Space Complexity: Recursive algorithms may require additional stack space for function calls.

Conclusion

The Divide and Conquer paradigm is a versatile and effective approach to algorithm design. By recursively breaking down problems into manageable pieces, it simplifies complex problems while often improving performance. From sorting to searching and beyond, its applications are foundational to computer science and computational problem-solving.

7.3. Parallelization of Numerical Problems

Parallelizing numerical problems is a critical technique in scientific computing and data analysis, enabling efficient solutions to computationally expensive tasks. By dividing large numerical computations across multiple processors or cores, parallelization reduces execution time and improves performance.

Types of Numerical Problems Suited for Parallelization

Matrix Operations:

Tasks such as matrix multiplication, inversion, and decomposition are highly parallelizable.
Libraries like NumPy, SciPy, and CuPy support parallel matrix computations.

Numerical Integration:

Parallelization helps break the integration range into smaller subranges for concurrent computation.

Example: Parallelizing Monte Carlo integration.

Differential Equations:

Solving systems of ordinary or partial differential equations (ODEs/PDEs) can benefit from domain decomposition techniques.

Linear Algebra:

Problems like solving linear systems or eigenvalue computations are amenable to parallelization.
Libraries like BLAS, LAPACK, and MPI-based tools are widely used.

Optimization Problems:

Parallel processing accelerates tasks like gradient computation or grid-based search in parameter optimization.

Fourier Transforms:

Fast Fourier Transform (FFT) computations, commonly used in signal processing, can be efficiently parallelized.

Techniques for Parallelizing Numerical Problems

Task Parallelism:

Divides tasks into independent units that can be executed concurrently.
Example: Each thread processes a specific subset of data.

Data Parallelism:

Distributes data across multiple processors, with each processor performing the same operation on its subset.
Example: Element-wise operations on large arrays.
Domain Decomposition:

Breaks the problem domain into subdomains for parallel processing.
Example: Finite element methods in PDE solving.

Tools and Libraries

NumPy:

Supports vectorized operations that internally utilize multithreading for speed.

Example:
python
Copy code
import numpy as np

```python
a = np.random.rand(1000, 1000)
b = np.random.rand(1000, 1000)
result = np.dot(a, b)    # Optimized parallel matrix multiplication
```

Multiprocessing:

Enables parallelism by distributing tasks across multiple cores.
Example:
python
Copy code

```python
from multiprocessing import Pool

def compute_square(x):
    return x ** 2

data = range(10)
with Pool(4) as pool:
    results = pool.map(compute_square, data)
print(results)
```

Joblib:

Simplifies parallel loops and shared memory access.

Example:
python
Copy code
```python
from joblib import Parallel, delayed

results = Parallel(n_jobs=4)(delayed(lambda x: x**2)(i) for i in range(1000))
print(results)
```

Dask:

Scales computation across multicore systems or clusters.
Example:
python
Copy code
import dask.array as da

x = da.random.random((10000, 10000), chunks=(1000, 1000))
result = (x @ x.T).compute()
print(result)

MPI (Message Passing Interface):

Used for distributed computing across nodes in a cluster.
Example: Using mpi4py for parallel numerical simulations.

GPU Computing:

Libraries like CuPy and PyCUDA enable parallel computation on GPUs.

Example:
python
Copy code
```python
import cupy as cp

a = cp.random.rand(1000, 1000)
b = cp.random.rand(1000, 1000)
result = cp.dot(a, b)  # Parallel GPU computation
```

Challenges in Parallelizing Numerical Problems

Load Balancing:

Ensuring all processors are equally utilized to avoid bottlenecks.

Communication Overhead:

Minimizing data transfer between processes or nodes to reduce latency.

Precision and Stability:

Maintaining numerical accuracy in parallel computations.

Scalability:

Ensuring algorithms perform well as the number of processors increases.

Debugging:

Debugging parallel code can be complex due to nondeterministic execution.

Applications

Climate Modeling:

Parallel solvers for large-scale PDEs in atmospheric simulations.

Particle Physics:

Parallel Monte Carlo simulations for high-energy particle interactions.

Machine Learning:

Accelerating matrix computations and optimization algorithms.

Image Processing:

Parallel FFT for large-scale image filtering and analysis.

Financial Modeling:

Speeding up option pricing and risk analysis using parallel Monte Carlo methods.

By using the right techniques and tools, parallelization of numerical problems can unlock significant computational power, making it a cornerstone of modern high-performance computing.

7.4. Load Balancing and Task Distribution

Load balancing and task distribution are critical concepts in parallel computing, ensuring optimal utilization of computational resources. They involve distributing work across multiple processors or cores to minimize execution time, reduce idle resources, and maximize efficiency.

Load Balancing

Load balancing refers to evenly distributing workloads among available processing units (threads, cores, or nodes). Proper load balancing prevents some processors from being overburdened while others remain underutilized.

Types of Load Balancing

Static Load Balancing:

Tasks are divided and assigned before execution begins.
Suitable when workloads and execution times are predictable.
Example: Dividing matrix rows equally among processors in matrix multiplication.

Dynamic Load Balancing:

Tasks are distributed during runtime based on processor availability.
Useful for irregular or unpredictable workloads.
Example: Assigning tasks to idle processors in a heterogeneous system.

Task Distribution

Task distribution determines how workloads are divided and assigned to processors. Effective task distribution minimizes inter-process communication and ensures each processor completes its tasks efficiently.

Task Distribution Strategies

Round-Robin Distribution:

Tasks are assigned cyclically to processors.
Simple and works well for uniform tasks.

Domain Decomposition:

The problem domain (e.g., a dataset or simulation grid) is divided into smaller regions, each assigned to a processor.
Common in numerical simulations like solving PDEs.

Work Queue:

Tasks are placed in a queue and assigned to processors as they become idle.
Dynamic and flexible for heterogeneous systems.

Master-Worker Model:

A central master process assigns tasks to worker processes and collects results.
Suitable for centralized control and management.

Factors Influencing Load Balancing and Task Distribution

Task Granularity:

Fine-grained tasks (small tasks): High overhead due to frequent communication.
Coarse-grained tasks (large tasks): Lower communication overhead but may lead to imbalance.

Resource Heterogeneity:

Different processors may have varying speeds and capabilities. Load balancing should account for this.

Task Dependencies:

Tasks that depend on the results of others require careful scheduling to avoid delays.

Communication Overhead:

Excessive communication between processors can negate the benefits of parallelism.

Workload Predictability:

Static strategies work well for predictable workloads; dynamic strategies are better for unpredictable tasks.

Load Balancing Techniques

Task Scheduling:

Algorithms like First Come, First Served (FCFS), Shortest Job First (SJF), and Priority Scheduling help allocate tasks efficiently.

Work Stealing:

Idle processors "steal" tasks from overloaded processors' queues.

Graph Partitioning:

Represents tasks and dependencies as a graph. Algorithms (e.g., METIS) partition the graph to balance workloads.

Load Monitoring:

Systems monitor resource usage and reassign tasks dynamically as needed.

Tools for Load Balancing and Task Distribution

MPI (Message Passing Interface):

Supports task distribution in distributed-memory systems.

Example:
python
Copy code
from mpi4py import MPI

```
comm = MPI.COMM_WORLD
rank = comm.Get_rank()
size = comm.Get_size()

data = [i for i in range(100)]
chunk_size = len(data) // size
chunk = data[rank * chunk_size:(rank + 1) * chunk_size]
print(f"Processor {rank} processing {chunk}")
```

Dask:

Automatically handles task distribution and scheduling for parallel workloads.

Example:
python
Copy code
```
import dask.array as da

x = da.random.random((10000, 10000), chunks=(1000, 1000))
result = x.sum().compute()
```

```python
print(result)
```

Ray:

Provides scalable distributed task execution.

Example:

```python
Copy code
import ray

ray.init()

@ray.remote
def task(x):
    return x ** 2

results = ray.get([task.remote(i) for i in range(10)])
print(results)
```

Load Balancers for Clusters:

Tools like Kubernetes and Apache Mesos manage workload distribution in cluster environments.

Challenges in Load Balancing

Scalability:

Ensuring the strategy works effectively as the number of processors grows.

Communication Overhead:

Balancing tasks without excessive data transfer between processors.

Heterogeneous Systems:

Adapting strategies for systems with varying hardware and network capabilities.

Dynamic Workloads:

Handling tasks that change in size or complexity during execution.

Applications

Web Servers:

Load balancers like HAProxy distribute incoming requests across multiple servers.

Scientific Simulations:

Distributing grid-based computations in climate models or fluid dynamics.

Big Data Processing:

Frameworks like Apache Hadoop and Spark distribute tasks across clusters for large-scale data analysis.

Game Engines:

Balancing workloads between CPUs and GPUs to ensure smooth gameplay.

Effective load balancing and task distribution are essential for optimizing resource utilization and achieving high performance in parallel computing systems.

7.5. Performance Profiling and Optimizing Parallel Code

Parallel computing can significantly speed up computational tasks, but poorly implemented parallel code may underperform or even degrade system performance. Performance profiling and optimization are crucial steps to ensure the code runs efficiently and takes full advantage of parallel resources.

Performance Profiling

Performance profiling involves analyzing a program to identify bottlenecks, inefficiencies, and areas for improvement. In parallel code, profiling focuses on resource utilization, synchronization overhead, and communication delays.

Key Metrics in Profiling Parallel Code

Execution Time:

Total time taken by the program to complete.
Helps identify the slowest sections.

Speedup:

Ratio of execution time of sequential code to parallel code.

Speedup
=
T
sequential
T
parallel
Speedup=
T

parallel

T
sequential

Efficiency:

Measures how effectively processors are utilized.

Efficiency
=
Speedup
Number of Processors
Efficiency=
Number of Processors
Speedup

Scalability:

How well the program performs as the number of processors increases.

Idle Time:

Time processors spend waiting due to load imbalance or synchronization.

Communication Overhead:

Time spent on inter-process communication.

Tools for Profiling Parallel Code

Python Profiling Tools:

cProfile:
Built-in Python module for profiling.

Example:
python
Copy code

```python
import cProfile

def parallel_task():
    # Parallel code here
    pass

cProfile.run('parallel_task()')
```
line_profiler:

Profiles code line by line.

memory_profiler:

Monitors memory usage.

Parallel-Specific Profiling Tools:

Intel VTune:

Profiles CPU, threading, and memory for high-performance code.

mpiP:

Lightweight profiling for MPI programs.

gprof:

General-purpose profiler for performance analysis.

nvprof:

Profiles GPU code using CUDA.

Visualization Tools:

SnakeViz:

Visualizes profiling data from cProfile.

Paraver:

Visualizes traces for performance analysis in parallel environments.

Optimizing Parallel Code

Optimization aims to improve the efficiency and performance of parallel programs by addressing bottlenecks and ensuring effective utilization of resources.

Strategies for Optimizing Parallel Code

Minimize Synchronization Overhead:

Reduce the frequency and duration of locks, barriers, and other synchronization mechanisms.

Balance the Load:

Use dynamic load balancing strategies to prevent idle processors.

Optimize Communication:

Minimize data transfer between processors.
Use shared memory for local communication and reduce network latency in distributed systems.

Increase Task Granularity:

Avoid overly fine-grained tasks that introduce significant overhead.
Aim for coarse-grained tasks with minimal inter-dependencies.

Use Efficient Libraries:

Leverage optimized libraries like NumPy, SciPy, Dask, and MPI for parallel operations.

Avoid False Sharing:

Ensure threads do not frequently access the same cache line, leading to performance degradation.

Optimize Memory Access:

Use contiguous data structures to exploit spatial locality.
Avoid unnecessary memory allocations.

Utilize Vectorization:

Exploit SIMD (Single Instruction, Multiple Data) instructions for faster computation.

Parallelism-Specific Optimizations

Threaded Code:

Avoid the Global Interpreter Lock (GIL) in Python by using multiprocessing or external libraries.

Example:

```python
Copy code
from multiprocessing import Pool

def task(x):
    return x**2

with Pool(4) as pool:
    results = pool.map(task, range(10))
```

Distributed Code:

Use Dask or Ray for efficient task scheduling and workload distribution.

Example:
python
Copy code
```
import dask.array as da

x = da.random.random((1000, 1000), chunks=(100, 100))
result = x.sum().compute()
print(result)
```

GPU Code:

Use libraries like CuPy or PyTorch for GPU acceleration.

Example:
python
Copy code
```
import cupy as cp
```

```
a = cp.random.rand(1000, 1000)
result = cp.dot(a, a)
```

Common Challenges in Parallel Optimization

Amdahl's Law:

Limits speedup based on the fraction of the code that cannot be parallelized.

Speedup

$\leq$

1

(

1

$-$

P

)

+

P

N

Speedup$\leq$

$(1-P)+$

N

P

1

P

P: Proportion of parallelizable code.

N

N: Number of processors.

Load Imbalance:

Uneven distribution of tasks leads to idle processors.

Deadlocks and Race Conditions:

Synchronization issues in multithreaded environments.

Scalability Limits:

Adding processors may not always lead to performance gains due to overhead.

Case Study: Optimizing Matrix Multiplication

Sequential Code:

```python
Copy code
import numpy as np

a = np.random.rand(1000, 1000)
b = np.random.rand(1000, 1000)
result = np.dot(a, b)
```

Parallel Code (Using Dask):

```python
Copy code
import dask.array as da

a = da.random.random((1000, 1000), chunks=(250, 250))
b = da.random.random((1000, 1000), chunks=(250, 250))
```

```python
result = da.dot(a, b).compute()
```

Optimized GPU Code:

```python
Copy code
import cupy as cp

a = cp.random.rand(1000, 1000)
b = cp.random.rand(1000, 1000)
result = cp.dot(a, b)
```

Conclusion

Profiling and optimizing parallel code are iterative processes that involve identifying bottlenecks, applying targeted improvements, and re-evaluating performance. With the right tools and techniques, developers can achieve significant speedups and scalability, ensuring their programs fully leverage parallel computing resources.

Chapter 8
High-Performance Computing with Python's

High-Performance Computing (HPC) involves leveraging powerful computing systems to solve complex problems that require significant computational resources. Python, with its simplicity and extensive ecosystem of libraries, has become a popular choice for HPC applications.

Key Aspects of Python in HPC

Parallel Computing:

Python supports parallelism via libraries like:
multiprocessing: For multi-core processing.
mpi4py: For distributed computing with MPI.
Dask: Scales computations across clusters.

GPU Computing:

Python enables GPU acceleration using:

CuPy and PyCUDA: GPU-accelerated array computations.

TensorFlow and PyTorch: For deep learning and large-scale numerical tasks.

Optimized Libraries:

Libraries like NumPy, SciPy, and Pandas are optimized for fast computations and can handle large datasets.

Distributed Computing:

Frameworks like Ray and Apache Spark simplify distributed task execution and big data processing.

Interfacing with Compiled Code:

Python integrates with high-performance languages (C, C++, Fortran) using tools like Cython, Numba, or F2Py, ensuring performance-critical parts run at native speeds.

Job Scheduling:

Python integrates with HPC schedulers like SLURM and PBS, enabling efficient resource management in cluster environments.

Applications

Scientific Simulations: Solving complex models in physics, chemistry, and biology.
Machine Learning: Training large-scale models using GPU clusters.
Data Analytics: Processing and analyzing massive datasets.
Engineering: Simulations in fluid dynamics, structural analysis, and more.

Example: Matrix Multiplication with Dask
python
Copy code

```python
import dask.array as da
```

```
# Create random arrays
a  =  da.random.random((10000,  10000),  chunks=(1000,
1000))
b  =  da.random.random((10000,  10000),  chunks=(1000,
1000))

# Perform matrix multiplication
result = da.dot(a, b).compute()
print(result)
```

Python's versatility and extensive libraries make it an excellent choice for HPC, enabling researchers and developers to build scalable, high-performance solutions.

8.1. Introduction to High-Performance Computing

High-Performance Computing (HPC) refers to the use of supercomputers, clusters, and powerful computing techniques to solve complex problems that require substantial computational power. HPC systems are designed to perform billions or trillions of calculations per second, enabling breakthroughs in science, engineering, and business.

Key Features of HPC

Massive Parallelism:

HPC systems utilize thousands to millions of processing units working concurrently to execute tasks faster.

Scalability:

HPC environments can scale computations across multiple nodes, cores, or GPUs to handle growing workloads.

High-Speed Interconnects:

Specialized networks (e.g., InfiniBand) ensure low-latency communication between processors.

Large-Scale Data Handling:

HPC systems process and store massive datasets efficiently, often leveraging distributed file systems like Lustre or GPFS.

Components of HPC

Supercomputers:

High-end machines like Summit, Fugaku, and Frontier capable of petascale or exascale computations.

Clusters:

Groups of interconnected computers working together to solve computational
problems.

Middleware:

Software frameworks like MPI, OpenMP, and CUDA that enable parallel programming and resource management.

Schedulers:

Tools like SLURM or PBS ensure optimal allocation of computational tasks.

Applications of HPC

Scientific Research:

Simulating complex phenomena such as climate models, astrophysics, and molecular dynamics.
.

Engineering:

Solving computational fluid dynamics (CFD), structural analysis, and optimization problems.

Machine Learning and AI:

Training large-scale neural networks for image recognition, natural language processing, and autonomous systems.

Healthcare:

Genomic analysis, drug discovery, and medical imaging.

Finance:

High-frequency trading, risk analysis, and predictive modeling.

Benefits of HPC

Faster Problem Solving:

Reduces computation time from days to hours or minutes.

Complex Problem Handling:

Enables solving problems too large for traditional systems.

Innovation:

Drives advancements in science, technology, and industry.

Challenges in HPC

Cost:
Building and maintaining HPC systems is resource-intensive.

Scalability:

Ensuring applications scale efficiently with more processors.

Energy Consumption:

High operational power requirements.

Programming Complexity:

Developing efficient parallel code requires expertise.

Conclusion

High-Performance Computing is a cornerstone of modern technological and scientific progress, enabling the resolution of challenges that were once thought insurmountable. With ongoing advancements in hardware and software, HPC continues to expand its role in diverse fields, from fundamental research to practical applications.

8.2. Using Python for Scientific Computing

Python has become a leading language for scientific computing due to its simplicity, flexibility, and a rich ecosystem of libraries tailored for numerical analysis, data processing, and visualization. It empowers scientists and engineers to perform complex computations efficiently while maintaining code readability.

Key Advantages of Python in Scientific Computing
Ease of Use:

Python's intuitive syntax and readability make it accessible to non-programmers, enabling faster prototyping and experimentation.

Extensive Libraries:

A wide range of libraries provides pre-built functions and tools for specialized scientific tasks.

Interoperability:

Python can interface with C, C++, Fortran, and other languages, allowing the integration of legacy code and performance-critical components.

Community Support:

An active and growing community ensures continuous development and abundant resources for learning and troubleshooting.

Popular Libraries for Scientific Computing

Numerical Computing:

NumPy:

Core library for numerical operations and array processing.
Example:
python
Copy code
import numpy as np

a = np.array([1, 2, 3])
b = np.array([4, 5, 6])
result = np.dot(a, b) # Dot product
print(result)

SciPy:

Builds on NumPy for advanced mathematical functions, optimization, and signal processing.

Data Manipulation:

Pandas:

Efficient handling of structured data (e.g., DataFrames).
Example:
python
Copy code
import pandas as pd

```
data = {"x": [1, 2, 3], "y": [4, 5, 6]}
df = pd.DataFrame(data)
print(df.mean())  # Compute column-wise mean
```

Visualization:

Matplotlib:
For creating static, interactive, and animated plots.

Seaborn:
High-level interface for statistical data visualization.

Symbolic Mathematics:

SymPy:
Supports symbolic computation and algebra.

Example:
python
Copy code
from sympy import symbols, solve

```python
x = symbols('x')
solution = solve(x**2 - 4, x)
print(solution)
```

Parallel and Distributed Computing:

Dask:

Handles large datasets and parallel computations.
mpi4py:

Enables parallel processing using MPI.

Machine Learning:

Scikit-learn:

Machine learning algorithms for scientific data analysis.
TensorFlow and PyTorch:
For deep learning and GPU-accelerated computation.

Specialized Libraries:

Astropy: Astronomy-related computations.
Biopython: Bioinformatics tools.
NetworkX: Network analysis.

Applications of Python in Scientific Computing

Numerical Simulations:

Modeling physical systems, solving differential equations, and conducting Monte Carlo simulations.

Data Analysis:

Processing and analyzing large-scale experimental or observational data.

Visualization:

Creating detailed plots, graphs, and animations for better insights.

Optimization:

Solving complex optimization problems in engineering and operations research.

Machine Learning:

Training models for predictions, classifications, and data-driven insights.

Case Study: Solving a Differential Equation

python

```
Copy code
from scipy.integrate import solve_ivp
import matplotlib.pyplot as plt

# Define a differential equation: dy/dt = -2y
def dydt(t, y):
    return -2 * y

# Solve the equation with initial condition y(0) = 1
solution = solve_ivp(dydt, [0, 5], [1], t_eval=np.linspace(0,
5, 100))

# Plot the solution
plt.plot(solution.t, solution.y[0])
plt.xlabel("Time")
plt.ylabel("y")
plt.title("Solution of dy/dt = -2y")
plt.show()
```

Challenges and Limitations

Performance:

Python's interpreted nature makes it slower than compiled languages for certain tasks. Libraries like Numba and Cython mitigate this issue.

Memory Management:

Handling very large datasets can be challenging in memory-constrained systems.

Dependency Management:

Managing multiple dependencies can be cumbersome without tools like virtual environments or package managers.

Conclusion

.

Python has revolutionized scientific computing, providing an accessible yet powerful platform for research and innovation. With its extensive ecosystem and continuous evolution, Python remains a versatile tool for solving complex scientific problems, from theoretical modeling to data-driven discoveries.

8.3. Integrating Python with C/C++ for Performance

Python is renowned for its simplicity and productivity but often falls short in compute-intensive scenarios due to its interpreted nature. By integrating Python with C/C++, developers can leverage the raw performance of these compiled languages while maintaining Python's ease of use. This hybrid approach is ideal for high-performance applications in fields like scientific computing, image processing, and machine learning.

Why Integrate Python with C/C++?

Enhanced Performance:

C/C++ executes operations much faster than Python, especially for complex algorithms and large datasets.

Reuse of Existing Code:

Many high-performance libraries and legacy systems are written in C/C++ and can be reused seamlessly.

Hardware Access:

C/C++ provides low-level hardware access, enabling fine-grained control for tasks like memory management and parallel processing.

Custom Optimizations:

Developers can implement performance-critical components directly in C/C++ for optimized execution.

Common Techniques for Integration

1. Using Cython

Cython is a Python-like language that compiles to C, enabling faster execution.

It allows embedding C code and converting Python functions to C equivalents.

Example:

```python
Copy code
# Save as example.pyx
def multiply(int a, int b):
    return a * b
```

Compile and Use:

```bash
Copy code
cythonize -i example.pyx
```

```python
Copy code
import example
print(example.multiply(3, 4))  # Outputs: 12
```

2. Using ctypes

ctypes is a Python library for calling C functions in shared libraries.
Example:

```c
// Save as example.c
int add(int a, int b) {
    return a + b;
}
```

Compile:

```bash
gcc -shared -o example.so -fPIC example.c
```

Python Usage:

```python
Copy code
```

```python
import ctypes
lib = ctypes.CDLL('./example.so')
result = lib.add(3, 5)
print(result)  # Outputs: 8
```

3. Using pybind11

A modern C++ library that simplifies binding C++ code to Python.
Provides a clean interface for integrating Python and C++.

Example:

cpp
Copy code

```cpp
#include <pybind11/pybind11.h>

int add(int a, int b) {
    return a + b;
}

PYBIND11_MODULE(example, m) {
```

```cpp
    m.def("add", &add, "A function that adds two
numbers");
}
```
Compile:

```bash
bash
Copy code
c++ -O3 -shared -std=c++17 -fPIC $(python3 -m pybind11
--includes) example.cpp -o example$(python3-config
--extension-suffix)
```

Python Usage:

```python
python
Copy code
import example
print(example.add(10, 20)) # Outputs: 30
```

4. Using the Python C API

Write Python extensions in C for direct integration with
Python's runtime.
Example:

```c
Copy code
#include <Python.h>

static PyObject* add(PyObject* self, PyObject* args) {
    int a, b;
    if (!PyArg_ParseTuple(args, "ii", &a, &b))
        return NULL;
    return PyLong_FromLong(a + b);
}

static PyMethodDef methods[] = {
    {"add", add, METH_VARARGS, "Add two numbers"},
    {NULL, NULL, 0, NULL}
};

static struct PyModuleDef module = {
    PyModuleDef_HEAD_INIT, "example", NULL, -1,
methods
};

PyMODINIT_FUNC PyInit_example(void) {
```

```
    return PyModule_Create(&module);
}
```

Compile and Use:

bash
Copy code
```
gcc -shared -o example.so -fPIC $(python3-config
--cflags --ldflags) example.c
```
python
Copy code
```
import example
print(example.add(2, 3))  # Outputs: 5
```

Applications

Numerical Computing:

Speed up linear algebra, matrix operations, or simulations using custom C/C++ algorithms.

Machine Learning:

Implement low-level operations like tensor manipulations or model optimization in C++ for frameworks like PyTorch or TensorFlow.

Image Processing:

Accelerate tasks like image filtering and edge detection using optimized C++ functions.

Data Analysis:

Process large-scale data efficiently with native C/C++ libraries.

Best Practices

Profile Before Optimization:

Use Python profilers (e.g., cProfile, line_profiler) to identify bottlenecks before integrating C/C++.

Start Small:

Optimize only performance-critical sections of code with C/C++ to avoid unnecessary complexity.

Test Thoroughly:

Validate the integrated system for correctness and stability across various scenarios.

Memory Management:

Be cautious about memory leaks and ensure proper cleanup in C/C++.

Use Modern Tools:

Favor libraries like pybind11 or Cython for easier integration and maintainability.

Conclusion

Integrating Python with C/C++ is a powerful way to achieve both productivity and performance. By combining Python's high-level capabilities with the speed of C/C++, developers can create scalable, efficient, and feature-rich applications for diverse fields like scientific research, AI, and engineering.

8.4. GPU Programming with Python

GPU (Graphics Processing Unit) programming leverages the massive parallelism of modern GPUs to accelerate computationally intensive tasks. With Python's high-level simplicity and specialized libraries, GPU programming has become accessible for tasks in fields like machine learning, scientific simulations, and image processing.

Why Use GPUs?

Massive Parallelism:

GPUs have thousands of cores designed to perform parallel computations, making them ideal for tasks like matrix operations and data processing.

High Throughput:

GPUs handle large-scale computations more efficiently than CPUs for tasks involving high data concurrency.

Specialized Hardware:

GPUs are optimized for floating-point arithmetic, which is critical for simulations, rendering, and AI applications.

Scalability:

Many systems support multiple GPUs, enabling further scaling of computational workloads.

Applications of GPU Programming

Machine Learning:

Accelerating neural network training and inference (e.g., TensorFlow, PyTorch).

Scientific Simulations:

Simulating physical systems, molecular dynamics, and climate models.

Image and Signal Processing:

Tasks like image filtering, object detection, and Fourier transforms.

Cryptography:

Speeding up algorithms like hashing and encryption.

Financial Modeling:

Risk analysis, Monte Carlo simulations, and high-frequency trading.
GPU Programming Frameworks in Python

1. CuPy

A NumPy-like library optimized for GPU computations.

Provides familiar syntax, making it easy to migrate existing NumPy code to GPUs.

Example:

```python
Copy code
import cupy as cp

# Create GPU arrays
x = cp.array([1, 2, 3])
y = cp.array([4, 5, 6])

# Perform operations
z = cp.dot(x, y)
print(z)  # Outputs: 32
```

2. Numba

A JIT (Just-In-Time) compiler for Python that enables GPU acceleration.
Requires minimal changes to existing Python code.

Example:

```python
Copy code
from numba import cuda

@cuda.jit
def add_arrays(x, y, result):
    idx = cuda.grid(1)
    if idx < x.size:
        result[idx] = x[idx] + y[idx]

# Data
import numpy as np
n = 100000
x = np.arange(n)
y = np.arange(n)
result = np.zeros(n)
```

```python
# Transfer to GPU
add_arrays[n//256, 256](x, y, result)
print(result[:10])  # Outputs first 10 results
```

3. PyCUDA

Provides a Python interface for NVIDIA's CUDA API.

Allows detailed control over GPU resources.

Example:

```python
python
Copy code
import pycuda.autoinit
import pycuda.driver as drv
import numpy as np
from pycuda.compiler import SourceModule

# CUDA kernel
mod = SourceModule("""
__global__ void double_array(float *a) {
```

```
    int idx = threadIdx.x + blockIdx.x * blockDim.x;
    a[idx] *= 2;
}
""")

func = mod.get_function("double_array")

# Data
a = np.random.randn(256).astype(np.float32)
func(drv.InOut(a), block=(256, 1, 1), grid=(1, 1))
print(a)
```

4. TensorFlow and PyTorch

Both frameworks provide high-level APIs for GPU acceleration, especially for deep learning.

Example with TensorFlow:

```
python
Copy code
import tensorflow as tf
```

```
# Run operation on GPU
with tf.device('/GPU:0'):
    a = tf.constant([1.0, 2.0, 3.0])
    b = tf.constant([4.0, 5.0, 6.0])
    result = tf.tensordot(a, b, axes=1)
print(result)  # Outputs: 32.0
```

Challenges in GPU Programming

Data Transfer Overhead:

Transferring data between CPU and GPU can be a bottleneck.

Memory Management:

GPUs have limited memory compared to CPUs, requiring careful memory allocation.

Debugging Complexity:

Debugging GPU kernels is harder due to limited tooling and parallel execution.

Device Compatibility:

Ensuring compatibility with different GPUs and drivers can be challenging.

Learning Curve:

Understanding GPU architectures and parallel programming paradigms requires additional effort.

Best Practices for GPU Programming

Optimize Data Transfers:

Minimize CPU-GPU data transfers to reduce latency.

Use Libraries:

Leverage existing libraries like CuPy and Numba for common operations to save development time.

Profile and Optimize:

Use profiling tools like NVIDIA Nsight or PyCUDA's built-in profiler to identify bottlenecks.

Batch Operations:

Group operations to fully utilize GPU resources.

Scalability:

Design code to scale across multiple GPUs if needed.

Conclusion

GPU programming with Python bridges the gap between high-level productivity and low-level performance. With tools like CuPy, Numba, and PyCUDA, Python makes GPU acceleration accessible to developers and researchers, enabling breakthroughs in computational science, AI, and engineering. By understanding GPU architecture and leveraging Python's robust ecosystem, developers can unlock unprecedented performance for their applications.

8.5. Optimizing Code for Multicore Architectures

Modern multicore processors offer significant potential for improving the performance of compute-intensive applications by enabling parallel execution of tasks. However, to leverage this potential, developers must optimize their code to efficiently utilize the available cores and manage parallel execution effectively.

Key Principles of Multicore Optimization

Parallelism:

Identify portions of code that can run concurrently and divide them into independent tasks.

Load Balancing:

Distribute work evenly across cores to prevent bottlenecks caused by idle resources.

Minimizing Overheads:

Reduce the overhead associated with task creation, synchronization, and communication.

Efficient Data Sharing:

Use shared resources judiciously and minimize contention between threads.

Approaches to Optimize Code

1. Task Decomposition

Break the problem into smaller, independent tasks that can be executed in parallel.

Examples:

Splitting loops into chunks for parallel execution.
Dividing data structures like arrays or matrices for processing by different cores.

Example:

python
Copy code
```
import multiprocessing

def process_data(data_chunk):
    # Perform computation
    return sum(data_chunk)

data = list(range(1000000))
chunk_size = len(data) // multiprocessing.cpu_count()
chunks = [data[i:i + chunk_size] for i in range(0, len(data), chunk_size)]

with multiprocessing.Pool() as pool:
    results = pool.map(process_data, chunks)
print(sum(results))
```

2. Threading

Use threads to run tasks concurrently on multiple cores. Python's threading module allows lightweight threading, though limited by the Global Interpreter Lock (GIL) for CPU-bound tasks.

Example:

```python
Copy code
import threading

def worker(data):
    # Perform some computation
    print(f"Processing {data}")

threads = []
for i in range(4):  # Number of threads
    t = threading.Thread(target=worker, args=(i,))
    threads.append(t)
    t.start()
```

```
for t in threads:
    t.join()
```

Note: For CPU-bound tasks, use multiprocessing instead of threading to bypass the GIL.

3. Multiprocessing

Python's multiprocessing module creates separate processes for parallel execution, bypassing the GIL and fully utilizing multiple cores.

Example:

python
Copy code
```python
from multiprocessing import Pool

def compute_square(x):
    return x * x

numbers = list(range(10))
with Pool() as pool:
```

```
    results = pool.map(compute_square, numbers)
print(results)
```

4. Vectorization

Use vectorized operations to process data in bulk using libraries like NumPy or pandas.
This approach minimizes the overhead of loop-based execution and leverages multicore optimizations in underlying libraries.

Example:

python
Copy code
```
import numpy as np

data = np.arange(1000000)
result = data * 2  # Vectorized operation
```

5. Parallel Libraries

Utilize high-performance libraries that are already optimized for multicore architectures.

Examples include:

NumPy: For numerical computations.
Pandas: For data analysis.
Dask: For distributed computing.
Ray: For scalable parallel processing.

Techniques to Enhance Performance

1. Minimize Synchronization Overheads

Avoid excessive use of locks and synchronization primitives, as they can serialize tasks and degrade performance.

Example:

```python
Copy code
from threading import Lock
```

```
lock = Lock()
shared_resource = 0

def safe_increment():
    global shared_resource
    with lock:
        shared_resource += 1
```

2. Memory Access Optimization

Reduce contention for shared memory and utilize cache-friendly data structures.

Example:

Use contiguous arrays instead of linked lists for better cache locality.

3. Profile and Analyze

Use profiling tools to identify bottlenecks and hotspots in your code.

Tools include:

cProfile and line_profiler for Python.
OS-level profilers like top or perf.

Challenges in Multicore Optimization

Task Dependency:

Some tasks may have dependencies that limit their ability to execute in parallel.

Load Imbalance:

Uneven task distribution can lead to cores being underutilized.

Overheads:

Excessive creation of threads/processes and synchronization can reduce the benefits of parallelism.

Debugging Complexity:

Identifying and fixing bugs in parallel code can be more challenging than in sequential code.

Best Practices

Start Simple:

Begin by identifying the most computationally expensive parts of your code and parallelizing them.

Use Existing Libraries:

Leverage libraries like NumPy, Dask, and multiprocessing to avoid reinventing parallel solutions. Profile Before Optimizing:

Identify performance bottlenecks to focus optimization efforts effectively.

Test Thoroughly:

Parallel execution introduces race conditions and deadlocks that require careful testing.

Conclusion

Optimizing code for multicore architectures is essential to achieve significant performance improvements in modern applications. By employing parallel programming techniques such as threading, multiprocessing, and vectorization, and by leveraging optimized libraries, developers can fully utilize multicore CPUs. However, careful consideration of task dependencies, synchronization, and profiling is necessary to maximize efficiency and maintain code correctness.

Chapter 9

Distributed Computing with Python

Distributed computing involves using multiple interconnected systems to solve computational problems collaboratively. Python provides a rich ecosystem for implementing distributed systems, making it a popular choice for scaling applications and processing large datasets across multiple machines.

Key Benefits

Scalability: Handle larger workloads by distributing tasks across multiple nodes.

Fault Tolerance: Systems can recover from individual node failures.

Resource Optimization: Utilize resources like memory, CPU, and storage across a cluster.

Popular Python Libraries for Distributed Computing

1. Dask

Provides a parallel computing framework for handling large-scale data.

Integrates seamlessly with NumPy, pandas, and scikit-learn.

Example:

```python
Copy code
import dask.array as da

x = da.random.random((10000, 10000), chunks=(1000, 1000))
result = x.mean().compute()
```

```python
print(result)
```

2. Ray

Simplifies distributed applications by abstracting low-level details.
Useful for machine learning and reinforcement learning.
Example:

```python
python
Copy code
import ray

ray.init()

@ray.remote
def compute_square(x):
    return x * x

futures = [compute_square.remote(i) for i in range(4)]
results = ray.get(futures)
print(results)
```

3. PySpark

Python API for Apache Spark, ideal for big data processing and analytics.
Example:

```python
Copy code
from pyspark.sql import SparkSession

spark = SparkSession.builder.appName("example").getOrCreate()
data = spark.read.csv("data.csv")
data.show()
```

4. Celery

A task queue for executing asynchronous jobs distributed across workers.
Example:

```python
Copy code
```

```python
from celery import Celery

app = Celery('tasks', broker='redis://localhost:6379/0')

@app.task
def add(x, y):
    return x + y
```

Challenges

Communication Overheads: Synchronization and data transfer between nodes can slow performance.
Fault Management: Handling node failures gracefully requires robust designs.
Debugging Complexity: Distributed systems are harder to debug due to their asynchronous nature.

Best Practices

Design for Parallelism: Break tasks into independent units.
Use Fault-Tolerant Frameworks: Leverage libraries like Ray or Spark for resilience.

Monitor Performance: Use monitoring tools to track resource utilization and identify bottlenecks.

Conclusion

Python's libraries like Dask, Ray, PySpark, and Celery simplify building distributed applications, making it easier to process large-scale data and achieve high performance. By addressing challenges like synchronization and fault tolerance, Python enables scalable, efficient, and reliable distributed systems.

9.1. Introduction to Distributed Systems

A distributed system is a collection of independent computers that appear to users as a single coherent system. These systems collaborate to perform tasks, share resources, and communicate over a network to achieve a common goal. Distributed systems are foundational in modern computing, powering everything from cloud services and web applications to large-scale data processing platforms.

Key Characteristics of Distributed Systems
Decentralization:

The system consists of multiple nodes, with no single point of control.

Concurrency:

Multiple processes run concurrently across different machines.

Scalability:

Nodes can be added or removed dynamically to scale the system up or down.

Fault Tolerance:

The system continues to function even if some components fail.

Transparency:

Users interact with the system as if it were a single entity, regardless of its distributed nature.

Components of a Distributed System

Nodes:

Independent machines (physical or virtual) participating in the system.

Communication:

Mechanisms like message passing, RPC (Remote Procedure Call), or REST APIs enable nodes to exchange data.

Coordination:

Algorithms and protocols ensure consistency, synchronization, and efficient task distribution.

Middleware:

Software that provides common services like communication, security, and resource management across nodes.

Types of Distributed Systems

Client-Server Systems:

Clients request services, and servers respond.
Example: Web applications.

Peer-to-Peer Systems:

All nodes are equal and share resources without a central authority.
Example: File-sharing networks like BitTorrent.

Distributed Databases:

Systems that store data across multiple locations while ensuring consistency.

Example: Apache Cassandra.

Cloud Computing Platforms:

Provide on-demand computing resources over the internet.
Example: Amazon AWS, Google Cloud.

Advantages of Distributed Systems

Resource Sharing:

Utilize resources across multiple nodes efficiently.

Scalability:

Scale horizontally by adding more nodes to the system.

Fault Tolerance:

Redundancy and replication ensure system reliability.

Performance:

Distribute workloads to achieve faster processing and lower latency.

Challenges in Distributed Systems

Network Reliability:

Communication delays or failures can disrupt operations.

Consistency:

Maintaining data consistency across nodes is challenging.

Fault Handling:

Designing systems to recover from partial failures is complex.

Security:

Protecting data and communications across a distributed network requires robust measures.

Applications of Distributed Systems

Web Services:

Power large-scale platforms like Google Search, Facebook, and Netflix.

Big Data Processing:

Analyze massive datasets using frameworks like Apache Hadoop and Spark.

Blockchain:

Secure and decentralized ledgers for cryptocurrencies and smart contracts.

IoT Systems:

Enable interconnected devices to communicate and share data.

Conclusion

Distributed systems are critical for modern applications that require scalability, fault tolerance, and high performance. While they introduce challenges like managing consistency and handling failures, advancements in distributed algorithms and technologies continue to make these systems more robust and efficient. By understanding their principles and design, developers can build systems that power everything from cloud computing to real-time applications.

9.2. Dask: Parallel Computing on Large Datasets

Dask is a flexible parallel computing library in Python designed to scale computations from a single machine to a distributed cluster. It is particularly well-suited for handling large datasets that exceed the memory capacity of a single machine, offering seamless integration with familiar Python libraries like NumPy, pandas, and scikit-learn.

Key Features of Dask

Scalability:

Works efficiently on small datasets and scales to large datasets using distributed clusters.

Familiar Syntax:

Provides drop-in replacements for NumPy arrays, pandas DataFrames, and scikit-learn estimators.

Lazy Evaluation:

Builds computation graphs and executes them only when the result is needed, optimizing resource usage.

Parallel Execution:

Breaks tasks into smaller chunks and processes them concurrently.

Fault Tolerance:

Resilient to worker failures, especially in distributed settings.

Core Components of Dask

Dask Arrays:

Parallel and distributed counterparts of NumPy arrays.

Example:

python
Copy code
```python
import dask.array as da

# Create a Dask array
x = da.random.random((10000, 10000), chunks=(1000, 1000))
result = x.mean().compute()   # Compute the mean in parallel
print(result)
```

Dask DataFrames:

Parallelized pandas DataFrames for large-scale data analysis.

Example:

python
Copy code
```python
import dask.dataframe as dd
```

```python
# Read a large CSV file
df = dd.read_csv("large_dataset.csv")
result   =   df.groupby("column").sum().compute()      # Compute grouped sum
print(result)
```

Dask Bags:

Handle unstructured data similar to Python lists but in parallel.

Example:

python
Copy code
```python
import dask.bag as db

data = db.from_sequence([1, 2, 3, 4, 5])
result = data.map(lambda x: x ** 2).compute() # Compute square of elements
print(result)
```

Dask Delayed:

Enables custom parallel computations by building computation graphs manually.

Example:

```python
Copy code
from dask import delayed

@delayed
def add(x, y):
    return x + y

result = add(1, 2) + add(3, 4)
print(result.compute())  # Outputs: 10
```

Dask Scheduler:

Coordinates task execution across threads, processes, or distributed clusters.

Advantages of Dask for Large Datasets

Out-of-Core Computing:

Processes datasets that don't fit into memory by working on smaller chunks.

Integration with Ecosystem:

Extends existing libraries like NumPy, pandas, and scikit-learn to handle larger datasets.

Dynamic Task Scheduling:

Optimizes execution plans dynamically based on available resources.

Cluster Support:

Scales from a single laptop to a distributed cluster effortlessly.

Applications of Dask

Big Data Analysis:

Analyze large datasets stored in formats like CSV, Parquet, or HDF5.

Machine Learning:

Train models on large datasets by integrating Dask with scikit-learn or XGBoost.

Scientific Computing:

Perform large-scale simulations or data processing.

ETL Pipelines:

Efficiently extract, transform, and load data across distributed environments.

Challenges of Using Dask

Learning Curve:

Understanding lazy evaluation and computation graphs may require time.

Debugging:

Debugging parallel code is inherently more complex than sequential code.

Cluster Management:

Setting up and managing distributed clusters can be challenging for beginners.

Best Practices

Profile Your Code:

Use Dask's built-in profiling tools to identify bottlenecks.

Optimize Chunk Sizes:

Choose chunk sizes that balance computation and memory overhead.

Monitor Resources:

Use Dask's web-based dashboard to monitor performance and resource utilization.

Leverage Existing Functions:

Use Dask's optimized methods for common operations instead of writing custom ones.

Conclusion

Dask is a powerful tool for parallel and distributed computing in Python, enabling users to scale familiar workflows to handle large datasets. With its integration into Python's data ecosystem and support for both single-machine and distributed environments, Dask simplifies big data analysis and high-performance computing for researchers and developers alike.

9.3. Celery: Task Queues and Distributed Task Processing

Celery is an open-source, distributed task queue system that is widely used for executing asynchronous and scheduled jobs. It enables developers to run time-consuming tasks, such as sending emails, processing images, or performing database updates, in the background, freeing up the main application to handle user requests more efficiently.

Key Features of Celery

Asynchronous Execution:

Allows tasks to be executed in the background without blocking the main application.

Distributed Processing:

Tasks can be executed across multiple worker nodes for scalability and fault tolerance.

Flexible Backends:

Supports various message brokers like RabbitMQ, Redis, and Amazon SQS.

Scheduling:

Enables periodic task execution using libraries like celery-beat.

Extensibility:

Integrates seamlessly with Python web frameworks such as Flask and Django.

How Celery Works

Producer:

The application that sends tasks to the task queue.

Broker:

A message broker (e.g., Redis or RabbitMQ) stores and routes tasks to workers.

Worker:

A process that listens for tasks, retrieves them from the broker, and executes them.

Result Backend:

Stores the results of completed tasks, enabling users to retrieve and monitor outputs.

Setting Up Celery

Install Celery and a Broker:

bash
Copy code

pip install celery[redis]

Define a Celery Application:

```python
Copy code
from celery import Celery

app = Celery('tasks', broker='redis://localhost:6379/0')

@app.task
def add(x, y):
    return x + y
```

Run a Worker:

```bash
Copy code
celery -A tasks worker --loglevel=info
```

Send Tasks:

```python
Copy code
from tasks import add
```

```
result = add.delay(4, 6)
print(result.get())  # Outputs: 10
```

Scheduling Tasks

Using the celery-beat extension, you can schedule tasks to run periodically.

Install celery-beat:

bash
Copy code
```
pip install celery[redis] celery-beat
```

Configure the Scheduler:

Add a schedule in your Celery configuration and use the periodic task interface to run tasks at regular intervals.

Common Use Cases

Background Jobs:

Processing user uploads, generating reports, or sending emails.

Real-Time Workflows:

Executing jobs in response to user actions or system events.

ETL Pipelines:

Extract, transform, and load data across distributed systems.

Distributed Machine Learning:

Parallelize model training or data preprocessing tasks.

Benefits of Celery

Improved Performance:

Frees up the main application for handling user interactions while tasks execute in the background.

Scalability:

Easily add workers to process tasks concurrently.

Fault Tolerance:

Automatically retries failed tasks, ensuring reliability.

Extensive Ecosystem:

Works seamlessly with various message brokers, web frameworks, and task scheduling tools.

Challenges of Celery

Setup Complexity:

Requires setting up a broker and managing workers.

Monitoring:

While tools like Flower provide task monitoring, configuring them can be an additional effort.

Concurrency Management:

Optimizing the number of workers and threads can be challenging for high loads.

Best Practices

Choose the Right Broker:

Redis is simpler to configure, while RabbitMQ is better for high-throughput systems.

Use Idempotent Tasks:

Design tasks to handle retries gracefully without duplicating effects.

Monitor and Debug:

Use tools like Flower or custom dashboards to track task performance and failures.

Optimize Worker Configuration:

Adjust worker concurrency and prefetch settings to balance throughput and resource usage.

Conclusion

Celery is a powerful tool for handling asynchronous and distributed task processing, enabling developers to offload time-consuming operations and scale applications efficiently. Its flexible architecture and rich ecosystem make it suitable for a wide range of use cases, from simple background jobs to complex distributed workflows. While it introduces some complexity in setup and management, following best practices ensures robust and scalable implementations.

9.4. Building Distributed Applications with Pyro4

Pyro4 (Python Remote Objects) is a library that simplifies the creation of distributed applications by enabling communication between Python objects across a network. It abstracts the complexities of network communication, allowing developers to focus on the application logic while Pyro4 handles the underlying details of remote procedure calls (RPCs), serialization, and object management.

Key Features of Pyro4

Object-Oriented Approach:

Interact with remote objects as if they were local.

Transparent Communication:

Handles serialization and deserialization of Python objects seamlessly.

Dynamic Object Location:

Automatically locates and communicates with remote objects using a name server.

Secure Communication:

Supports authentication and encryption for secure data transfer.

Scalability:

Facilitates the creation of distributed systems with multiple servers and clients.

How Pyro4 Works

Remote Objects:

Pyro4 allows you to expose Python objects over the network.

Name Server:

Acts as a directory for remote objects, simplifying object discovery.

Proxy Objects:

Used by clients to interact with remote objects.

Serialization:

Automatically converts Python objects into a transmittable format.
Getting Started with Pyro4

Install Pyro4:

bash
Copy code
pip install Pyro4

Create a Remote Object:

python
Copy code

```python
import Pyro4

@Pyro4.expose
class Calculator:
    def add(self, x, y):
        return x + y


daemon = Pyro4.Daemon()  # Create a Pyro daemon
uri = daemon.register(Calculator)    # Register the Calculator class
print(f"Ready. Object URI: {uri}")
daemon.requestLoop()  # Start the event loop
```

Run a Name Server:

bash
Copy code

```bash
python -m Pyro4.naming
```

Register the Object with the Name Server:

python
Copy code

```python
import Pyro4

@Pyro4.expose
class Calculator:
    def add(self, x, y):
        return x + y

daemon = Pyro4.Daemon()
ns = Pyro4.locateNS()  # Locate the Name Server
uri = daemon.register(Calculator)
ns.register("example.calculator", uri)    # Register the object with the Name Server
print("Calculator is ready.")
daemon.requestLoop()
```

Create a Client to Use the Remote Object:

python
Copy code
```python
import Pyro4

# Locate the remote object
```

```
calculator                                           =
Pyro4.Proxy("PYRONAME:example.calculator")

# Call the remote method
result = calculator.add(10, 20)
print(f"The result is {result}")
```

Advantages of Using Pyro4

Ease of Use:

Simple API for exposing and accessing remote objects.

Pythonic Design:

Object-oriented approach aligns well with Python developers' workflows.

Dynamic Scalability:

Adding or removing components is straightforward with the Name Server.

Customizability:

Supports hooks for custom serialization, logging, and connection handling.

Challenges and Limitations

Python-Specific:

Pyro4 is tailored for Python, which limits its use in polyglot environments.

Network Latency:

Performance depends on network speed, making it unsuitable for high-frequency, low-latency applications.

Concurrency Management:

Developers must handle concurrency in the application logic if required.

Manual Configuration:

Setting up Name Servers and managing object lifecycles can be tedious.

Applications of Pyro4

Distributed Systems:

Build systems where components interact over a network, such as microservices or distributed databases.

Remote Monitoring:

Implement systems to monitor and control remote devices or processes.

Data Processing Pipelines:

Distribute computation tasks across multiple nodes.

Education and Prototyping:

Use Pyro4 to demonstrate concepts of distributed computing and networked systems.

Best Practices

Use a Name Server:

Register objects with the Name Server to simplify client interactions.

Enable Security:

Use Pyro4's SSL support for secure communication.

Optimize Serialization:

Ensure custom objects are efficiently serializable to minimize overhead.

Monitor Performance:

Profile the system for bottlenecks, especially in high-latency networks.

Conclusion

Pyro4 makes it straightforward to build distributed systems by abstracting network communication and providing an intuitive, object-oriented API. While it is best suited for Python-centric environments and applications that don't require extreme performance, it remains a powerful tool for prototyping, teaching, and building scalable distributed systems.

9.5. Using MPI for Python (mpi4py)

mpi4py is a Python library that provides bindings for the Message Passing Interface (MPI), a standardized and portable framework for parallel computing. It enables developers to write high-performance, distributed applications by leveraging MPI's efficient communication protocols for processes running on multiple nodes.

Key Features of mpi4py

Interoperability:

Provides access to the MPI API while integrating seamlessly with Python.

Scalability:

Supports distributed computing on clusters of thousands of processors.

Ease of Use:

Offers a Pythonic interface for complex MPI operations like point-to-point and collective communication.

Rich Functionality:

Includes features for sending/receiving data, broadcasting, scattering, gathering, and parallel I/O.

Getting Started with mpi4py

Installation:

bash
Copy code
pip install mpi4py

Basic Example:

python
Copy code
from mpi4py import MPI

comm = MPI.COMM_WORLD   # The default communicator
rank = comm.Get_rank() # Get the process ID (rank)
size = comm.Get_size()   # Get the total number of processes

```python
print(f"Hello from process {rank} out of {size}")
```

Run the script using mpiexec or mpirun:

bash
Copy code
```
mpiexec -n 4 python script.py
```
Output:

csharp
Copy code
```
Hello from process 0 out of 4
Hello from process 1 out of 4
Hello from process 2 out of 4
Hello from process 3 out of 4
```

Communication Patterns in mpi4py

Point-to-Point Communication:

Used for direct data transfer between two processes.

Send and Receive Example:

python

Copy code

```python
if rank == 0:
    data = {"key": "value"}
        comm.send(data, dest=1, tag=11)   # Send data to process 1
elif rank == 1:
    data = comm.recv(source=0, tag=11)   # Receive data from process 0
    print(f"Received {data} at process 1")
```

Collective Communication:

Used for communication among all processes in a group.

Broadcast Example:

python

Copy code

```python
if rank == 0:
    data = "Hello, MPI!"
else:
```

```
data = None
```
data = comm.bcast(data, root=0) # Broadcast data from root (0)
print(f"Process {rank} received data: {data}")

Scatter Example:

python
Copy code
```
if rank == 0:
    data = [1, 2, 3, 4]
else:
    data = None
data = comm.scatter(data, root=0)  # Distribute elements
print(f"Process {rank} received {data}")
```

Gather Example:

python
Copy code
```
data = rank  # Each process contributes its rank
result = comm.gather(data, root=0)  # Gather data at root
if rank == 0:
```

```
print(f"Gathered data: {result}")
```

Advanced Features of mpi4py

Parallel I/O:

Perform efficient input/output operations on large datasets distributed across processes.

Custom Data Types:

Define and use custom MPI data types for complex data structures.

Inter-Communicators:

Enable communication between separate groups of processes.

Shared Memory:

Facilitate efficient communication between processes on the same node.

Applications of mpi4py

Scientific Simulations:

Simulate physical phenomena like fluid dynamics or climate modeling.

Large-Scale Data Processing:

Process and analyze massive datasets distributed across clusters.

Machine Learning:

Distribute training workloads for deep learning models.

Graph and Network Analysis:

Perform computations on large-scale graphs or social networks.

Advantages of mpi4py

High Performance:

Leverages the underlying MPI implementation for efficient communication.

Portability:

Works on any platform with an MPI implementation (e.g., OpenMPI, MPICH).

Ease of Learning:

Simplifies the complex MPI API into a Python-friendly interface.

Flexibility:

Supports both synchronous and asynchronous communication patterns.

Challenges of mpi4py

Steep Learning Curve:

Understanding parallel programming concepts like deadlocks and race conditions is essential.

Debugging Complexity:

Debugging distributed applications can be challenging due to concurrency.

Dependency on MPI:

Requires a working MPI installation, which may involve additional setup.

Limited Python Integration:

While efficient, Python's Global Interpreter Lock (GIL) can limit performance in multi-threaded scenarios.

Best Practices

Minimize Communication Overhead:

Group smaller messages into larger ones and use collective operations where possible.

Balance Workloads:

Ensure that workloads are evenly distributed to avoid bottlenecks.

Profile Performance:

Use tools like mpiP or Tau to identify performance bottlenecks.

Handle Faults Gracefully:

Incorporate mechanisms to recover from process or node failures.

Conclusion

mpi4py brings the power of MPI to Python, enabling developers to build high-performance distributed applications. Its ease of use and Pythonic interface make it an excellent choice for researchers and engineers working on scientific computing, large-scale simulations, and parallel data processing. While mastering mpi4py and parallel programming can be challenging, its scalability and performance make it a valuable tool in the distributed computing landscape.

Chapter 10
Debugging and Testing Parallel Code

Debugging and testing parallel code can be challenging due to the complexities of concurrency, non-deterministic behavior, and potential race conditions. Effective strategies and tools are essential to ensure correctness, performance, and scalability in parallel applications.

Challenges in Debugging Parallel Code

Non-Deterministic Behavior:

Results may vary between runs due to the order of thread or process execution.

Race Conditions:

Conflicts arise when multiple threads or processes access shared resources simultaneously.

Deadlocks:

Processes or threads may block each other indefinitely, halting the program.

Scalability Issues:

Bugs may only appear when scaling up to a large number of threads, processes, or nodes.
Strategies for Debugging Parallel Code

Reproducibility:

Use fixed random seeds or controlled scheduling to reproduce issues consistently.

Incremental Testing:

Test individual components or smaller subsets of the system before integrating them.

Debugging Tools:

Use tools like GDB, Valgrind, or TotalView for low-level debugging.
Utilize Python-specific tools such as PDB or PyCharm's debugger for parallel processes.

Logging and Tracing:

Implement extensive logging with timestamps, process IDs, and thread IDs.
Use tracing tools like Intel VTune or Arm Forge for detailed performance insights.

Static Analysis:

Leverage static code analysis tools to identify potential issues before runtime (e.g., Clang-Tidy or Coverity).

Thread-Safe Practices:

Ensure proper synchronization using locks, semaphores, or atomic operations.

Testing Parallel Code

Unit Testing:

Test individual threads or processes independently to validate logic.

Stress Testing:

Run the application under heavy workloads or with numerous processes to identify bottlenecks and race conditions.

Regression Testing:

Test previously fixed issues to ensure they don't reappear in newer code.

Automated Testing:

Use frameworks like pytest with extensions for parallel tests (e.g., pytest-xdist) to automate test execution.

Mocking Parallel Components:

Use mocks or simulators to test the behavior of components in isolation.

Best Practices

Start Simple: Debug with minimal parallelism (e.g., a single thread or process) before scaling up.

Test on Realistic Environments: Use production-like environments to identify issues specific to distributed systems.

Use Timeouts: Set timeouts for operations to detect and handle deadlocks.

Monitor Performance: Profile the application to detect inefficiencies or unexpected slowdowns.

Conclusion

Debugging and testing parallel code require systematic approaches and specialized tools to address the complexities of concurrency. By combining reproducibility, robust testing strategies, and modern debugging tools, developers can ensure their parallel applications are both correct and performant.

10.1. Common Pitfalls in Parallel Programming

Parallel programming introduces unique challenges that can lead to subtle bugs, inefficiencies, and incorrect behavior. Understanding common pitfalls is crucial for writing effective and robust parallel applications.

1. Race Conditions

Description: Occur when multiple threads or processes access shared resources without proper synchronization, leading to unpredictable results.

Example: Two threads updating a shared variable simultaneously can overwrite each other's changes.

Solution:
Use synchronization primitives like locks, semaphores, or atomic operations.
Avoid unnecessary shared state.

2. Deadlocks

Description: A situation where two or more threads/processes wait for each other to release resources, resulting in a program freeze.

Example: Thread A locks Resource 1 and waits for Resource 2, while Thread B locks Resource 2 and waits for Resource 1.

Solution:
Enforce a consistent lock acquisition order.
Use timeout mechanisms to detect and recover from deadlocks.

3. Load Imbalance

Description: Some threads or processes finish their tasks earlier than others, leaving resources underutilized.

Example: Uneven partitioning of data in data-parallel tasks can cause certain processes to handle more workload.

Solution:

Use dynamic scheduling or load balancing techniques.

Leverage frameworks like Dask or OpenMP for automatic load balancing.

4. Excessive Synchronization Overhead

Description: Overuse of synchronization mechanisms (e.g., locks or barriers) can degrade performance due to contention and blocking.

Example: Locking every access to a shared resource, even when unnecessary.

Solution:

Minimize synchronization regions.

Use fine-grained or reader-writer locks instead of coarse-grained locks.

5. False Sharing

Description: Occurs when multiple threads inadvertently modify variables that share the same cache line, causing frequent cache invalidations.
Example: Two threads updating separate elements of the same array can trigger false sharing.
Solution:
Align data structures to avoid cache line overlap.
Use padding to separate frequently accessed variables.

6. Insufficient Scalability

Description: The program does not scale well with increased resources due to bottlenecks or inefficiencies.
Example: A single thread handling critical sections can become a bottleneck in a multi-threaded application.
Solution:
Profile the application to identify bottlenecks.

Optimize communication patterns and reduce serialization points.

7. Lack of Reproducibility

Description: Non-deterministic behavior in parallel programs makes debugging and testing difficult.
Example: Results may vary across runs due to different thread execution orders.
Solution:
Use fixed random seeds for consistency.
Implement logging to trace execution paths.

8. Overhead of Communication

Description: Excessive communication between processes or threads can outweigh the benefits of parallelization.
Example: Distributed systems spending more time exchanging data than performing computations.

Solution:

Optimize communication patterns (e.g., use bulk data transfers).

Reduce data dependency between tasks.

9. Ignoring Memory Hierarchy

Description: Poor memory access patterns can lead to cache misses and degraded performance.

Example: Accessing non-contiguous memory blocks in a loop.

Solution:

Optimize data locality by accessing memory sequentially.

Use cache-aware algorithms.

10. Incorrect Granularity

Description: Tasks that are too small or too large can lead to inefficiencies.

Example: Splitting a simple computation into too many small tasks causes excessive overhead.

Solution:

Balance task granularity based on workload and system capabilities.

Use frameworks like ThreadPoolExecutor or MPI for optimal task distribution.

11. Poor Error Handling

Description: Ignoring errors in threads or processes can lead to silent failures or cascading issues.

Example: A failed worker process in a distributed system goes unnoticed.

Solution:

Implement robust error handling and monitoring mechanisms.

Use libraries or frameworks with built-in fault tolerance (e.g., Celery or Ray).

12. Overlooking Debugging and Testing

Description: Parallel bugs are often subtle and hard to reproduce, making them difficult to debug and test.

Example: Skipping stress testing for race conditions or deadlocks.

Solution:

Use specialized debugging tools like Intel Inspector or TotalView.

Write unit tests and integration tests to cover edge cases.

Conclusion

Parallel programming can significantly enhance performance but requires careful attention to detail to avoid common pitfalls. By understanding these challenges and adopting best practices, developers can build efficient, scalable, and reliable parallel applications.

10.2. Tools for Debugging Parallel Code

Debugging parallel code can be complex due to issues like race conditions, deadlocks, and non-deterministic behavior. Several specialized tools are designed to help developers identify and resolve these issues in multi-threaded and distributed applications.

1. Debuggers for Parallel Code
GDB (GNU Debugger)

Description: A powerful, open-source debugger for programs written in C, C++, and other languages.

Features:

Supports debugging of multi-threaded applications.
Allows inspection of thread-specific states.
Can integrate with MPI for distributed programs.
Usage:
bash
Copy code
gdb -np <num_processes> <program>

LLDB

Description: The debugger component of the LLVM project, designed for parallel applications.

Features:

Debugs multi-threaded and distributed applications.
Offers a user-friendly command-line interface.

Integration:

Works well with tools like OpenMP and MPI.
TotalView

Description: A commercial debugger tailored for parallel programming.

Features:

Supports multi-threaded, MPI, and GPU applications.
Provides graphical interfaces for visualizing parallel code execution.

Detects memory leaks and errors.

Use Case:
Ideal for large-scale HPC applications.

2. Profilers and Analyzers

Intel Inspector
Description: A tool for detecting memory and threading errors.

Features:
Identifies race conditions, deadlocks, and synchronization issues.

Supports multi-threaded and MPI-based applications.
Integration:

Works seamlessly with Intel compilers and parallel libraries.

Valgrind

Description: A framework for memory debugging, profiling, and error detection.

Tools:

Helgrind: Detects race conditions and threading bugs.
Memcheck: Identifies memory errors.

Use Case:
Debugging multi-threaded applications with memory safety issues.

Arm Forge (DDT)
Description: A commercial tool for debugging and profiling HPC applications.

Features:

Supports debugging MPI, OpenMP, and CUDA-based applications.
Provides a graphical interface for visualizing processes and threads.

Advantages:

Easy to use for large-scale distributed systems.

3. Thread and Concurrency Debugging Tools
Thread Sanitizer (TSan)
Description: A tool for detecting race conditions in multi-threaded applications.

Features:

Integrates with compilers like GCC and Clang.
Offers detailed error reports with stack traces.

Usage:
Compile the program with -fsanitize=thread to enable TSan.

PyInstrument

Description: A lightweight Python profiler for multi-threaded code.

Features:

Identifies slow sections in parallel Python applications.
Provides visual call graphs.
Debugging Libraries (Python):
pdb: Standard Python debugger.
faulthandler: Tracks crashes and timeouts in multi-threaded Python applications.

4. Specialized Parallel Debugging Tools

MPI-Specific Debuggers

MPICH and OpenMPI Debugging Utilities:

Offer logging and debugging options for MPI applications.
Can be combined with GDB or TotalView.
Coz (Causal Profiler)
Description: A performance profiler for multi-threaded code.

Features:

Identifies performance bottlenecks in parallel sections.
Suggests optimizations for improved scalability.

TAU (Tuning and Analysis Utilities)

Description: A comprehensive profiling and debugging tool for HPC applications.

Features:
Supports MPI, OpenMP, and hybrid parallel models.
Provides detailed performance metrics.

5. GPU Debugging Tools

NVIDIA Nsight
Description: A set of tools for debugging and profiling GPU applications.

Features:

Debugs CUDA and OpenCL applications.
Offers performance analysis for GPU kernels.

ROCm (AMD Debugging Tools)

Description: Tools for debugging parallel code on AMD GPUs.

Features:
Provides kernel profiling and debugging.

6. Distributed Debugging Tools

Log Aggregators
Elasticsearch/Kibana: Collect and visualize logs from distributed systems.
Graylog: Monitor logs across multiple nodes.
Jaeger
Description: A distributed tracing tool for monitoring parallel and distributed systems.

Features:

Tracks requests across multiple services.
Visualizes dependencies between components.

Best Practices for Debugging Parallel Code

Reproducibility:

Use fixed seeds and controlled environments to reproduce issues.

Incremental Testing:

Test smaller components before debugging the entire system.

Monitoring and Logging:

Implement detailed logging to trace execution paths.

Combine Tools:
Use a combination of debugging, profiling, and tracing tools for comprehensive analysis.

Conclusion

Debugging parallel code requires specialized tools to handle the complexities of concurrency and distributed systems. By leveraging tools like TotalView, Intel Inspector, and Valgrind, developers can efficiently detect and resolve bugs, ensuring the reliability and performance of parallel applications.

10.3. Writing Testable Parallel Code

Parallel programming introduces complexities like race conditions, deadlocks, and non-deterministic behavior, which can make testing more challenging. Writing testable parallel code requires adopting practices and techniques that simplify debugging, isolate issues, and ensure correctness in concurrent environments.

Key Principles for Testable Parallel Code
Modular Design:

Break the code into smaller, self-contained units with clear responsibilities.
Ensure each module can be tested independently.

Deterministic Behavior:

Avoid non-deterministic outcomes by controlling execution order where possible.
Use fixed random seeds for reproducibility during tests.

Clear State Management:

Minimize shared states between threads or processes.
Use thread-safe data structures and synchronization primitives to manage shared resources.

Separation of Concerns:

Keep parallel logic (e.g., thread/process management) separate from business logic.

This separation simplifies testing the core functionality without parallel overhead.

Error Handling:

Implement robust error handling to gracefully manage failures in parallel tasks.
Use logging to capture errors for debugging.

Best Practices for Writing Testable Parallel Code

Use Frameworks and Libraries:

Leverage high-level frameworks like Dask, Ray, or ThreadPoolExecutor for built-in parallelism and testing support.

Avoid Tight Coupling:

Design components to work independently to facilitate isolated testing.
Use mocking to simulate dependencies during unit tests.

Granularity Balance:

Ensure tasks are neither too small (causing excessive overhead) nor too large (reducing parallel efficiency).

Test Synchronization Mechanisms:

Validate that locks, barriers, and other synchronization tools are used correctly to avoid deadlocks and race conditions.

Implement Timeouts:

Use timeouts for blocking operations to detect and handle hangs during tests.

Testing Strategies for Parallel Code

Unit Testing:

Focus on individual components or functions.
Mock parallelism to test logic in isolation.
Example (Python with pytest):

```python
Copy code
from unittest.mock import patch

def parallel_function(data):
    return sum(data)

def test_parallel_function():
    with patch("module.parallel_function", return_value=10):
        result = parallel_function([1, 2, 3, 4])
        assert result == 10
```

Integration Testing:

Test interactions between components, including parallel execution.
Use small-scale parallelism to validate behavior before scaling.

Stress Testing:

Simulate high workloads to uncover bottlenecks, race conditions, or deadlocks.

Use tools like pytest-xdist to run tests concurrently.

Regression Testing:

Ensure changes to the codebase do not reintroduce resolved issues, especially in parallel sections.

Fuzz Testing:

Test parallel code with randomized inputs to uncover edge cases and unexpected behavior.

Tools for Testing Parallel Code

Testing Frameworks:

PyTest: Widely used for Python applications, supports parallel testing with plugins like pytest-xdist.

Unittest: A built-in Python library for writing test cases.

Concurrency Debugging Tools:

Thread Sanitizer (TSan): Detects race conditions and threading bugs.

Intel Inspector: Identifies memory and synchronization errors in parallel code.

Mocking Tools:

Use Python's unittest.mock module to simulate parallel components.

Performance Profilers:

Tools like cProfile, PyInstrument, or Valgrind help analyze performance and identify bottlenecks.

Example: Writing and Testing Parallel Code

Parallel Function:
python
Copy code
from concurrent.futures import ThreadPoolExecutor

```python
def compute_square(n):
    return n * n

def parallel_square(numbers):

    with ThreadPoolExecutor() as executor:
      results = executor.map(compute_square, numbers)
      return list(results)
```

Unit Test:
python
Copy code

```python
def test_compute_square():
    assert compute_square(4) == 16

def test_parallel_square():
    numbers = [1, 2, 3, 4]
    expected = [1, 4, 9, 16]
    result = parallel_square(numbers)
    assert result == expected
```

Common Challenges and Solutions

Non-Deterministic Tests:

Use fixed seeds or controlled execution for reproducible results.

Timing Dependencies:

Avoid tests that rely on specific execution timing; use explicit synchronization instead.

Test Environment Mismatch:

Simulate production-like environments during testing to catch deployment-specific issues.

Conclusion

Writing testable parallel code involves thoughtful design, modularity, and a focus on reproducibility. By leveraging modern tools, frameworks, and testing strategies, developers can ensure the correctness and reliability of parallel applications, even in complex multi-threaded or distributed environments.

10.4. Unit Testing and Profiling in Parallel Applications

Parallel applications present unique challenges in testing and performance optimization due to concurrency, shared state, and non-deterministic behavior. Effective unit testing and profiling are essential to ensure correctness and optimal performance.

Unit Testing in Parallel Applications

Key Objectives of Unit Testing

Validate the correctness of individual components.
Ensure thread/process safety.
Catch race conditions, deadlocks, and synchronization issues.

Challenges in Unit Testing Parallel Applications

Non-Determinism: Different thread execution orders can cause varying results.

Shared Resources: Multiple threads or processes accessing shared data can lead to inconsistent states.

Scalability Issues: Behavior may differ when running on a single core versus multiple cores or nodes.

Best Practices for Unit Testing Parallel Code

Test in Isolation:

Write tests for individual functions or components, avoiding dependencies on other threads or processes.

Mock Parallelism:

Use mocking to simulate parallel behavior in isolation. For Python, use the unittest.mock library.

Control Execution Order:

Use deterministic inputs and fixed random seeds to make tests reproducible.

Simulate Edge Cases:

Test scenarios such as high contention, resource starvation, or unexpected failures.

Automate Tests:

Use tools like pytest with plugins like pytest-xdist for running tests concurrently.

Example: Unit Testing a Parallel Function
python
Copy code

```python
from concurrent.futures import ThreadPoolExecutor

# Parallel function
def compute_square(n):
    return n * n
```

```python
def parallel_compute(numbers):
    with ThreadPoolExecutor() as executor:
        results = executor.map(compute_square, numbers)
    return list(results)

# Unit test
def test_parallel_compute():
    numbers = [1, 2, 3, 4]
    expected = [1, 4, 9, 16]
    assert parallel_compute(numbers) == expected
```

Profiling in Parallel Applications

Importance of Profiling

Profiling helps identify bottlenecks, inefficient resource usage, and suboptimal parallelism in applications. It provides insights into:

Thread/process performance.
CPU and memory usage.
Synchronization overhead.

Challenges in Profiling Parallel Applications

Granularity: Fine-grained profiling may introduce overhead, skewing results.

Non-Deterministic Behavior: Execution paths may differ across runs.

Distributed Systems: Profiling across multiple nodes requires specialized tools.

Best Practices for Profiling

Use Parallel-Aware Profilers:

Select tools that support threading, multiprocessing, and distributed systems.

Profile Specific Sections:

Focus on critical regions of code, such as hot loops or synchronization points.

Minimize Overhead:

Use sampling-based profilers to reduce performance impact.

Analyze Scalability:

Profile with varying numbers of threads or processes to identify scalability bottlenecks.

Tools for Profiling Parallel Applications

Python Profiling Tools:

cProfile: A built-in profiler for Python.
PyInstrument: Provides a graphical representation of execution time.
line_profiler: Profiles line-by-line execution.

System-Level Profilers:

Intel VTune: Optimizes threading and identifies bottlenecks.
Valgrind (Callgrind): Analyzes performance at the process level.

Perf: A Linux tool for analyzing CPU usage.

Distributed Profiling:

Dask Profiler: Profiles task graphs for parallel computing.
OpenMPI Tools: Analyzes MPI-based distributed systems.

Example: Profiling Parallel Code
python
Copy code

```python
import cProfile
import pstats
from io import StringIO

from concurrent.futures import ThreadPoolExecutor

# Function to profile
def compute_square(n):
    return n * n

def parallel_compute(numbers):
```

```python
    with ThreadPoolExecutor() as executor:
        results = executor.map(compute_square, numbers)
    return list(results)

# Profiling
pr = cProfile.Profile()
pr.enable()
parallel_compute([1, 2, 3, 4, 5])
pr.disable()

# Print profiling stats
s = StringIO()
sortby = 'cumulative'
ps = pstats.Stats(pr, stream=s).sort_stats(sortby)
ps.print_stats()
print(s.getvalue())
```

Integrating Unit Testing and Profiling

To ensure both correctness and performance:

Run unit tests under profiled environments to identify performance issues in functional code.

Use test frameworks that integrate with profilers, such as pytest-profiling.

Conclusion

Unit testing ensures correctness and thread/process safety in parallel applications, while profiling identifies and optimizes performance bottlenecks. Together, they form a comprehensive approach to developing robust and efficient parallel systems. By following best practices and leveraging the right tools, developers can build scalable, reliable, and high-performance applications.

Chapter 11

Best Practices for Parallel Python Programming

Parallel programming in Python can enhance performance by leveraging multi-threading, multiprocessing, or distributed systems. However, to ensure efficiency, reliability, and scalability, developers must follow best practices.

1. Choose the Right Parallel Model

Multi-threading: Suitable for I/O-bound tasks, leveraging Python's threading module.

Multiprocessing: Ideal for CPU-bound tasks, using the multiprocessing module to bypass the Global Interpreter Lock (GIL).

Asynchronous Programming: For high-concurrency I/O operations, use asyncio.

Distributed Computing: Leverage tools like Dask, Ray, or Celery for large-scale systems.

2. Minimize Shared State

Avoid shared resources between threads or processes to prevent race conditions.
Use thread-safe data structures or synchronization mechanisms like locks or queues.

3. Optimize Task Granularity

Ensure tasks are appropriately sized:
Too small: Overhead from task management reduces performance.
Too large: Parallelism is underutilized.

4. Profile and Benchmark

Identify bottlenecks using profilers like cProfile, line_profiler, or Intel VTune.
Benchmark parallel code under different workloads to assess scalability.

5. Handle Synchronization Carefully

Use primitives like locks, semaphores, and barriers to manage access to shared data.
Avoid excessive synchronization, which can degrade performance.

6. Test Parallel Code Thoroughly

Write deterministic and reproducible tests.
Use tools like pytest-xdist for concurrent test execution.
Test for edge cases like race conditions, deadlocks, and high contention.

7. Leverage High-Level Libraries

Use frameworks like ThreadPoolExecutor, ProcessPoolExecutor, or Dask to abstract low-level parallelism details.
For machine learning or GPU tasks, utilize TensorFlow, PyTorch, or CuPy.

8. Monitor Resource Usage

Monitor CPU, memory, and network usage to ensure efficient resource utilization.
Use system-level tools like top, htop, or Python's psutil.

9. Debug Parallel Code Effectively

Use tools like Thread Sanitizer or Intel Inspector to detect race conditions and threading issues.
Implement extensive logging to trace execution paths.

10. Scale Gradually

Start with a single thread or process, then scale up as needed.
For distributed systems, test scalability by incrementally increasing the number of nodes or workers.

Conclusion

Parallel Python programming requires careful design and testing to achieve optimal performance and correctness. By adhering to these best practices, developers can efficiently utilize parallelism to build scalable and reliable applications.

11.1. Optimizing for Performance

Performance optimization in Python involves improving execution speed, reducing resource usage, and ensuring scalability. For parallel and sequential applications, optimizations focus on efficient algorithms, effective resource utilization, and leveraging Python's ecosystem of libraries and tools.

1. Algorithm Optimization

Choose Efficient Algorithms: Select algorithms with lower time and space complexity.

Use Data Structures Wisely: Leverage appropriate data structures, such as dictionaries for fast lookups or sets for membership checks.

Avoid Redundant Calculations: Cache results using memoization or Python's functools.lru_cache.

2. Leverage Built-in Libraries

Use Python's standard library functions and modules, which are often written in optimized C.

Example: Use sum() instead of a manual loop for summation.

For numerical and scientific computations, use libraries like:

NumPy: For vectorized operations.

Pandas: For data manipulation.

SciPy: For advanced mathematical operations.

3. Optimize Parallelism

Understand the Task Type:

I/O-bound tasks: Use asyncio or threading.

CPU-bound tasks: Use multiprocessing or Cython to bypass the GIL.

Task Granularity: Ensure tasks are neither too small (high overhead) nor too large (limited parallelism).

Use high-level parallel libraries like Dask or Ray for distributed workloads.

4. Minimize Overhead

Avoid frequent context switching in multi-threading.

Use batch processing to reduce the overhead of frequent task creation.

5. Optimize Code Execution

Profile Before Optimizing: Identify bottlenecks using tools like:

cProfile: For general profiling.

line_profiler: For line-by-line analysis.

memory_profiler: For memory usage insights.

Hotspot Optimization: Focus on optimizing frequently executed sections.

Reduce Function Calls: Inline simple functions to avoid overhead.

6. Optimize Memory Usage

Avoid copying large data structures unnecessarily.
Use generators instead of lists for memory-efficient iterations.
Example:
python
Copy code

```python
# Memory-intensive list
squares = [x**2 for x in range(10**6)]
# Memory-efficient generator
squares = (x**2 for x in range(10**6))
```

Use specialized libraries like PyTorch or CuPy for memory-intensive GPU computations.

7. Compile Python Code

Use tools to convert Python to faster native code:
Cython: Write Python-like code that compiles to C.

Numba: JIT compilation for numerical functions.

PyPy: A just-in-time (JIT) compiler for Python.

8. Optimize I/O Operations

Use buffered I/O for frequent file operations.

For large datasets, prefer binary formats like HDF5 or Parquet over CSV.

Minimize network latency by batching requests or using asynchronous libraries.

9. Test and Scale

Stress Testing: Simulate real-world loads to ensure performance under peak conditions.

Scalability Testing: Gradually increase input size or resource usage to find bottlenecks.

10. Monitor and Iterate

Continuously monitor resource usage with tools like:

psutil: For CPU and memory monitoring.

Perf: For system performance metrics.

Regularly revisit code for optimizations, especially when scaling.

Conclusion

Performance optimization in Python is a multi-faceted process that combines efficient algorithms, resource management, and leveraging Python's ecosystem of tools. Profiling and iterative improvements are critical to ensuring that applications remain fast, efficient, and scalable.

11.2. Memory Management and Avoiding Memory Leaks

Memory management is a critical aspect of writing efficient and scalable Python applications. Although Python handles memory allocation and deallocation automatically through garbage collection, developers must still understand how to optimize memory usage and prevent memory leaks.

1. Understanding Memory Management in Python

Automatic Memory Management: Python uses a garbage collector to manage memory, which automatically frees unused memory.

Reference Counting: Python tracks the number of references to each object. When an object's reference count drops to zero, its memory is released.

Garbage Collection: Python's gc module identifies and cleans up cyclic references (e.g., circular data structures).

2. Common Causes of Memory Leaks

Unreleased Resources:

Open file handles, sockets, or database connections not properly closed.

Reference Cycles:

Circular references (e.g., two objects referencing each other) that the reference counting mechanism cannot clean up.

Global Variables:

Objects held in global scope that persist unnecessarily.

Caching:

Large or unnecessary objects stored in caches (e.g., functools.lru_cache without size limits).

Long-Lived Objects:

Objects in data structures like lists or dictionaries that are no longer needed but remain referenced.

3. Best Practices for Memory Management

Release Resources Properly

Use context managers (with statements) to ensure resources are released:

python

Copy code

```python
with open("file.txt", "r") as file:
    data = file.read()
```

Avoid Unnecessary References

Delete objects explicitly when they are no longer needed:

python

Copy code

```python
del obj
```

Limit Global Variables

Minimize the use of global variables to prevent unintended memory retention.

Use Weak References

Use the weakref module for objects that should not increase reference counts.

Monitor Memory Usage
Use tools like psutil and tracemalloc to track memory consumption.

4. Identifying and Fixing Memory Leaks

Using Python's Garbage Collector

Force garbage collection and inspect unreachable objects:
python
Copy code
```
import gc
gc.collect()
```

Analyzing Memory Usage

Use the tracemalloc module to track memory allocations:

```python
Copy code
import tracemalloc

tracemalloc.start()

# Code to analyze
snapshot = tracemalloc.take_snapshot()
print(snapshot.statistics("lineno"))
```

Debugging Tools

objgraph: Visualize object references to identify leaks.
memory_profiler: Profile memory usage line by line.

5. Avoiding Memory Leaks in Parallel Applications

Thread Safety: Ensure that threads or processes do not hold onto references longer than necessary.
Shared Memory: Manage shared data structures carefully in multiprocessing or distributed applications.

Cleanup Tasks: Use explicit cleanup functions for parallel workers or processes.

6. Example: Fixing a Memory Leak
Problem Code:

python
Copy code
```python
class Node:
    def __init__(self, value):
        self.value = value
        self.next = None

# Create a reference cycle
a = Node(1)
b = Node(2)
a.next = b
b.next = a
```
Fix:

Break the reference cycle explicitly:

python

```
Copy code
a.next = None
b.next = None
```

Conclusion

Effective memory management in Python involves understanding how memory allocation works, avoiding common pitfalls like reference cycles, and using tools to monitor and debug memory usage. By following best practices and leveraging Python's garbage collector, developers can ensure efficient memory utilization and prevent memory leaks.

11.3. Writing Scalable Parallel Code

Scalability in parallel programming refers to the ability of a program to handle increased workloads efficiently by utilizing more computational resources, such as CPU cores, threads, or distributed nodes. Writing scalable parallel code requires careful design to maximize resource utilization while minimizing overhead and bottlenecks.

Key Principles of Scalable Parallel Code

Divide and Conquer:

Break tasks into smaller, independent units that can execute in parallel.
Use fine-grained or coarse-grained tasks depending on the workload and resource availability.

Minimize Dependencies:

Avoid shared state or tightly coupled tasks to reduce synchronization overhead.
Use data partitioning techniques to minimize contention.

Balance the Workload:

Distribute tasks evenly across available resources to prevent some resources from being idle while others are overloaded.

Use dynamic scheduling or load-balancing mechanisms to adapt to varying task execution times.

Optimize Communication:

Reduce communication overhead between threads, processes, or nodes by batching data transfers or using efficient protocols.

In distributed systems, minimize network latency by colocating tasks and data.

Leverage Hardware:

Utilize all available CPU cores using multiprocessing or threading.

Exploit GPUs for highly parallelizable tasks with frameworks like CUDA, PyTorch, or TensorFlow.

Steps to Write Scalable Parallel Code

1. Choose the Right Parallelism Model

Shared Memory:
Use threads (threading) or multiprocessing (multiprocessing) for single-machine parallelism.

Distributed Memory:

Use libraries like Dask, Ray, or MPI (mpi4py) for multi-node parallelism.

Asynchronous Parallelism:

Use asyncio for high-concurrency I/O-bound tasks.

2. Profile and Identify Bottlenecks

Use profiling tools like cProfile, line_profiler, and Dask Profiler to identify slow or resource-intensive parts of the code.
Focus optimization efforts on hotspots.

3. Ensure Efficient Resource Utilization

Avoid underutilization or contention for resources by dynamically allocating tasks.

Use thread pools (ThreadPoolExecutor) or process pools (ProcessPoolExecutor) for task management.

4. Implement Load Balancing

Use task queues to dynamically assign work to idle threads or processes.

For distributed systems, use frameworks like Dask to balance workloads across nodes.

5. Minimize Synchronization Overhead

Use locks, barriers, and semaphores judiciously to avoid contention and deadlocks.

Prefer lock-free algorithms or data structures when possible.

6. Optimize Data Partitioning

Split large datasets into independent chunks for parallel processing.
Ensure partitions are small enough to fit in memory and large enough to reduce overhead.

7. Test and Debug Parallel Code

Use deterministic inputs and controlled environments to test scalability and correctness.
Employ debugging tools like PySnooper, objgraph, and gdb for parallel debugging.

Example: Writing Scalable Parallel Code
Task: Parallel Sum of a Large Array
python
Copy code

```python
from concurrent.futures import ProcessPoolExecutor

def sum_chunk(chunk):
    return sum(chunk)

def parallel_sum(array, chunk_size):
```

```python
# Split array into chunks
chunks = [array[i:i + chunk_size] for i in range(0,
len(array), chunk_size)]

# Use multiprocessing to compute the sum of chunks
with ProcessPoolExecutor() as executor:
    results = executor.map(sum_chunk, chunks)

# Combine results
return sum(results)

# Example usage
large_array = list(range(1_000_000))
result = parallel_sum(large_array, chunk_size=10_000)
print("Sum:", result)
```

Challenges in Scalability

Amdahl's Law:

The speedup of parallel code is limited by the sequential portion of the program. Optimize the serial parts to achieve better scalability.

Overhead:

Task creation, communication, and synchronization can negate parallelism benefits if not managed efficiently.

Resource Constraints:

Memory, CPU, or network limitations can hinder scalability.

Tools and Frameworks for Scalable Parallel Code

Multiprocessing: For multi-core parallelism on a single machine.

Dask: For scalable task scheduling and distributed computing.

Ray: For distributed applications with a focus on scalability.

MPI (mpi4py): For high-performance computing in distributed memory systems.

Apache Spark: For big data parallelism.

Conclusion

Scalable parallel code enables efficient use of resources as workloads increase. By following best practices like minimizing dependencies, balancing workloads, and optimizing communication, developers can build applications that handle increasing demands while maintaining performance. Profiling and iterative improvements are key to achieving scalability in real-world systems.

11.4. Handling Exceptions in Parallel Code

Exception handling in parallel code ensures that errors are detected, managed, and reported effectively without causing deadlocks, resource leaks, or inconsistent states. Since parallel code involves multiple threads, processes, or nodes executing concurrently, managing exceptions becomes more complex compared to sequential code.

Challenges in Parallel Exception Handling

.

Isolated Execution Contexts:

Each thread or process operates independently, making it hard to propagate exceptions to the main program or other parallel tasks.

Partial Failures:

Some tasks may fail while others continue executing, potentially leading to inconsistent states.

Resource Cleanup:

Failure to release locks, file handles, or other resources can cause deadlocks or resource exhaustion.

Error Propagation:

Ensuring that errors in one part of the code are effectively communicated and handled by the main application or parent thread.

Non-deterministic Behavior:

Timing-related issues in parallel programs can make debugging exceptions difficult.

Best Practices for Exception Handling in Parallel Code

1. Centralized Error Reporting

Collect exceptions from all threads or processes in a centralized location for consistent handling.

Example using concurrent.futures:

```python
Copy code
from concurrent.futures import ThreadPoolExecutor

def task(n):
    if n == 2:
```

```
    raise ValueError("An error occurred")
return n * n

with ThreadPoolExecutor() as executor:
    futures = [executor.submit(task, i) for i in range(5)]

    for future in futures:
        try:
            print(future.result())
        except Exception as e:
            print(f"Exception: {e}")
```

2. Graceful Shutdown

Use cleanup mechanisms to ensure resources are released:
Context managers (with statements) for automatic resource cleanup.
Explicit finalizers to handle termination signals gracefully.

3. Propagating Exceptions

Propagate exceptions to the main thread to stop execution or take corrective actions:

Use shared queues or specialized exception-handling frameworks to communicate errors.

4. Using Fault-Tolerant Patterns

For distributed systems, design tasks to retry automatically in case of transient failures.

Use libraries like Ray or Dask, which have built-in fault tolerance.

5. Implementing Partial Rollback

For systems that can encounter partial failures, design rollback mechanisms to undo completed actions if a failure occurs.

Tools and Techniques for Handling Exceptions

1. Multithreading

Use exception-safe threading libraries like concurrent.futures.

Capture and propagate exceptions from individual threads:

python
Copy code
```python
import threading

def thread_task():
    try:
        raise RuntimeError("Thread error")
    except Exception as e:
        print(f"Caught exception in thread: {e}")

thread = threading.Thread(target=thread_task)
thread.start()
thread.join()
```

2. Multiprocessing

Handle exceptions in worker processes using multiprocessing.Pool:

python

Copy code

```python
from multiprocessing import Pool

def process_task(n):
    if n == 2:
        raise ValueError("Process error")
    return n * n

with Pool(4) as pool:
        results = pool.map(process_task, range(5), chunksize=1)
    print(results)
```

3. Distributed Systems

Use libraries like Dask, Ray, or Celery that provide built-in exception handling and retries for distributed workloads.

Example: Exception Handling in Parallel Code

Using concurrent.futures for Threaded Tasks

python

Copy code

```python
from concurrent.futures import ThreadPoolExecutor, as_completed

def safe_task(n):
    if n == 2:
        raise ValueError("Task failed")
    return n * n

with ThreadPoolExecutor(max_workers=4) as executor:
    futures = [executor.submit(safe_task, i) for i in range(5)]

    for future in as_completed(futures):
        try:
            print(future.result())
        except Exception as e:
            print(f"Caught exception: {e}")
```

Key Takeaways

Isolate Failures: Ensure that a failure in one parallel task does not affect others unnecessarily.

Graceful Degradation: Allow the program to continue operating in a degraded state where possible.

Centralized Logging: Log all exceptions for debugging and auditing purposes.

Test Parallel Code: Use deterministic test cases and simulation environments to reproduce and debug exceptions effectively.

By designing parallel code with robust exception handling, developers can build reliable and maintainable applications that scale efficiently.

11.5. Documentation and Code Maintainability

Parallel programming introduces complexities that make proper documentation and maintainability essential. Clear documentation and well-structured code help developers understand, debug, and enhance parallel applications, ensuring long-term scalability and ease of collaboration.

1. Importance of Documentation and Maintainability

Simplifies Debugging: Parallel applications can have non-deterministic behavior, making it difficult to trace bugs without proper documentation.

Facilitates Team Collaboration: Teams working on complex projects benefit from shared knowledge and consistent coding practices.

Supports Scaling: Scalable code often requires modifications, and maintainable code ensures such changes can be implemented efficiently.

Ensures Knowledge Transfer: Proper documentation ensures that new developers can quickly understand the codebase.

2. Key Aspects of Documentation

a. Inline Code Comments

Add concise comments explaining the purpose of key sections or complex logic.

```python
Copy code
# Spawning multiple threads for parallel processing
with ThreadPoolExecutor() as executor:
    results = executor.map(compute_task, data_chunks)
```

b. Function and Class Docstrings

Use docstrings to describe the purpose, input parameters, return values, and exceptions for each function or class.

```python
Copy code
def parallel_sum(data_chunks):
    """

    Compute the sum of data chunks in parallel.

    Args:
```

data_chunks (list): A list of data chunks to be summed.

Returns:

int: The total sum of all chunks.
"""

pass

c. Document Parallel Design

Provide an overview of how parallelism is implemented in the code:

Concurrency Model: Threads, processes, or distributed nodes.

Task Distribution: How tasks are divided and assigned.

Synchronization Mechanisms: Use of locks, barriers, or queues.

Fault Tolerance: Error-handling strategies.

d. Configuration and Deployment Notes

Document environment dependencies, configuration files, and deployment steps, especially for distributed systems.

3. Practices for Code Maintainability

a. Modular Design

Break the code into small, reusable functions and classes.
Each module should have a single responsibility, adhering to the Single Responsibility Principle (SRP).

b. Consistent Coding Style

Follow a consistent style guide, such as PEP 8 for Python.
Use descriptive variable and function names to improve readability.

c. Use Parallel Libraries

.Leverage well-documented libraries like Dask, Ray, or multiprocessing, which abstract parallel complexities and enhance maintainability.

d. Error Handling and Logging

Implement robust error handling and logging mechanisms to capture runtime issues without manual intervention.

python

Copy code

```
try:
    result = compute_task(data)
except Exception as e:
    logger.error(f"Task failed: {e}")
```

e. Testability

Write unit tests for individual components.
Use frameworks like pytest or unittest to ensure parallel sections work as expected.

4. Tools for Improving Documentation and Maintainability

a. Documentation Generators

Use tools like Sphinx or pdoc to generate documentation from docstrings.

b. Static Analysis Tools

Tools like pylint, flake8, or mypy can catch style and type errors early.

c. Profiling and Monitoring

Integrate tools like cProfile or line_profiler for performance analysis and maintain efficiency over time.

d. Version Control

Use Git with clear commit messages and branching strategies for collaborative code management.

e. Code Reviews

Regularly review code to ensure adherence to best practices and to spot potential issues.

5. Example: Well-Documented Parallel Function
python
Copy code
from concurrent.futures import ProcessPoolExecutor

```python
def compute_factorial(n):
    """
    Compute the factorial of a number.

    Args:
        n (int): The number to compute the factorial for.

    Returns:
        int: The factorial of the input number.

    Raises:

        ValueError: If the input is negative.
```

481

```python
    """
    if n < 0:
        raise ValueError("Negative input is not allowed.")
    return 1 if n == 0 else n * compute_factorial(n - 1)

def parallel_factorial(numbers):
    """
    Compute factorials for a list of numbers in parallel.

    Args:

        numbers (list): List of integers to compute factorials
for.

    Returns:

        list: Factorials of the input numbers.
    """
    with ProcessPoolExecutor() as executor:
        results = list(executor.map(compute_factorial,
numbers))
    return results
```

```python
# Example usage
if __name__ == "__main__":
    numbers = [5, 10, 15]
    print(parallel_factorial(numbers))
```

6. Benefits of Good Documentation and Maintainability

Reduced Technical Debt: Avoids accumulating inefficiencies or difficult-to-maintain code.

Improved Performance: Well-maintained code is easier to profile and optimize.

Team Productivity: Enhances collaboration and knowledge sharing.

Future-Proofing: Ensures the codebase can adapt to new requirements or technologies.

Conclusion

Documentation and maintainability are critical for parallel programming, given its inherent complexity. By adhering to best practices, providing clear documentation, and designing modular, testable code, developers can create robust and scalable parallel applications that remain efficient and easy to manage over time.

Chapter 12

Case Studies and Applications

Parallel Python programming is widely applied across industries to improve performance, scalability, and efficiency. Below are key areas and case studies where parallel programming has made a significant impact:

1. Scientific Computing

Application: Climate modeling, molecular dynamics, and astrophysics simulations.

Case Study: NASA uses parallel Python libraries like mpi4py to simulate large-scale climate models, enabling faster predictions and data analysis.

2. Big Data Analytics

Application: Data preprocessing, machine learning, and real-time analytics.

Case Study: Organizations like Uber leverage Dask to process large datasets in parallel, reducing processing time for data pipeline tasks.

3. Machine Learning and AI

Application: Training deep learning models and hyperparameter tuning.
Case Study: Facebook employs PyTorch, which supports parallel computations on GPUs and CPUs, to train complex neural networks for image and speech recognition.

4. Financial Services

Application: Risk modeling, algorithmic trading, and fraud detection.
Case Study: Investment banks use Ray to parallelize portfolio risk calculations across distributed clusters, achieving near real-time results.

5. Bioinformatics

Application: Genomic data analysis and protein structure prediction.

Case Study: Genomics companies utilize multiprocessing and GPU-based parallelism to sequence DNA faster, enabling quicker discoveries in personalized medicine.

6. Game Development

Application: Real-time physics simulations and rendering.

Case Study: Game engines integrate parallel Python for rendering graphics and simulating physics across multiple cores, improving gameplay performance.

7. Web Scraping and Automation

Application: High-volume web scraping and task automation.

Case Study: Marketing firms employ asyncio to scrape thousands of websites concurrently, gathering data for market analysis within hours.

8. High-Performance Computing (HPC)

Application: Large-scale simulations in engineering and physics.

Case Study: CERN uses Python with MPI (mpi4py) to distribute workloads for particle collision simulations across supercomputers.

9. Video Processing

Application: Video encoding, transcoding, and streaming.

Case Study: Streaming platforms leverage FFmpeg with Python wrappers for parallel video transcoding, ensuring faster delivery of content to users.

10. E-commerce

Application: Recommender systems and real-time inventory updates.

Case Study: Amazon uses parallel processing for recommendation engines, which analyze user data in real-time to suggest products.

Conclusion

Parallel Python programming is a versatile tool for tackling computationally intensive tasks across various domains. By leveraging libraries like Dask, Ray, and PyTorch, developers can achieve significant performance improvements, enabling innovative solutions in industries like healthcare, finance, and AI.

12.1. Parallel Image Processing

Parallel image processing involves breaking down computationally intensive tasks, such as filtering, transformation, or object detection, into smaller sub-tasks that can be executed simultaneously across multiple processors or cores. This approach significantly speeds up processing times and is particularly useful for large-scale or real-time image processing applications.

Why Parallelize Image Processing?

.

Improved Performance:

Tasks like resizing, filtering, and applying transformations to large images or video frames benefit from parallel execution.
Scalability:

Allows handling of large datasets or real-time streaming by distributing the workload.

Real-Time Processing:

Essential for applications like facial recognition, augmented reality, and live video editing.

Techniques for Parallel Image Processing

1. Multi-Core Processing

Utilizes multiple CPU cores to divide and process image data simultaneously.

Example: Using Python's multiprocessing library.
python
Copy code

```python
from multiprocessing import Pool
from PIL import Image

def process_image(image_path):
    img = Image.open(image_path).convert("L")  # Convert to grayscale
    img = img.resize((100, 100))  # Resize the image
    img.save(f"processed_{image_path}")
    return f"processed_{image_path}"

image_files = ["image1.jpg", "image2.jpg", "image3.jpg"]
with Pool() as pool:
    results = pool.map(process_image, image_files)
```

```python
print("Processed images:", results)
```

2. GPU-Based Parallelism

Leverages the massive parallel processing power of GPUs for image processing tasks.
Libraries: PyTorch, TensorFlow, CUDA (via PyCUDA).
Example: Applying GPU acceleration with PyTorch for image transformations.

```python
Copy code
import torch
from torchvision import transforms
from PIL import Image

device = torch.device("cuda" if torch.cuda.is_available() else "cpu")

# Load an image
image = Image.open("image.jpg")

# Define transformations
```

```python
transform = transforms.Compose([
    transforms.Resize((128, 128)),
    transforms.ToTensor()
])

# Apply transformations on GPU
tensor_image = transform(image).to(device)
print("Image processed on:", device)
```

3. Distributed Processing

Distributes image processing tasks across multiple nodes in a cluster.
Libraries: Dask, Ray, Apache Spark.

Example: Using Dask for distributed image processing.

python
Copy code
```python
from dask import delayed, compute
from PIL import Image


@delayed
```

```python
def process_image(image_path):
    img = Image.open(image_path).convert("L")
    img = img.resize((100, 100))
    img.save(f"processed_{image_path}")
    return f"processed_{image_path}"

image_files = ["image1.jpg", "image2.jpg", "image3.jpg"]
results = [process_image(image) for image in image_files]
compute(*results)
```

Applications of Parallel Image Processing

Medical Imaging:

Accelerating tasks like CT scan analysis, MRI reconstruction, and X-ray processing.

Surveillance:

Real-time object and facial recognition for security applications.

Content Creation:

Efficient rendering, editing, and manipulation of high-resolution images and videos.

E-commerce:

Bulk image resizing, watermarking, and optimization for product catalogs.

Autonomous Vehicles:

Parallel processing for real-time lane detection, obstacle recognition, and scene segmentation.

Challenges in Parallel Image Processing

Data Partitioning:

Dividing image data into independent chunks without affecting task outcomes.

Synchronization Overheads:

Managing dependencies and synchronization between parallel tasks can impact performance.

Hardware Constraints:

Efficiently leveraging available hardware like GPUs and avoiding bottlenecks.

Scalability:

Ensuring that the system can handle increasing workloads without significant performance degradation.

Conclusion

Parallel image processing harnesses the power of modern multi-core CPUs, GPUs, and distributed systems to handle computationally demanding tasks efficiently. With tools like multiprocessing, Dask, and PyTorch, developers can process large datasets or enable real-time applications. Despite challenges like data partitioning and synchronization, parallel processing has become indispensable in fields like AI, healthcare, and video processing.

12.2. Real-time Data Processing Systems

Real-time data processing systems are designed to handle and analyze data as it is generated, allowing for immediate insights, decision-making, and actions. These systems are crucial for applications where processing time directly impacts performance, such as fraud detection, real-time analytics, or industrial monitoring. The core idea behind real-time systems is to minimize latency and provide near-instantaneous responses to incoming data streams.

Key Characteristics of Real-time Data Processing Systems

Low Latency:

Real-time data processing systems must respond to incoming data with minimal delay. Latency is measured from data generation to the time an action is taken based on that data, typically in milliseconds or seconds.

Continuous Stream Processing:

These systems handle continuous streams of data, processing data as it arrives rather than in batches, enabling immediate feedback.

Scalability:

The ability to scale horizontally is essential for managing large volumes of incoming data from diverse sources, such as IoT devices, social media streams, and sensor networks.

Fault Tolerance:

Real-time systems need to be robust, capable of recovering gracefully from failures to avoid data loss or disruption in processing.

Event-driven Architecture:

These systems often rely on an event-driven architecture, where actions are triggered by specific events, such as a sensor reading exceeding a threshold or a financial transaction.

Components of Real-time Data Processing Systems

Data Sources:

The origin of real-time data, which can include sensors, IoT devices, web logs, stock tickers, social media feeds, or transactional systems.

Data Ingestion:

Tools for collecting and buffering streaming data before it is processed. Common tools include Apache Kafka, Amazon Kinesis, and Apache Pulsar.

Stream Processing Frameworks:

These frameworks handle the core logic of processing data streams in real-time. Examples include:
Apache Flink: A powerful system for stateful stream processing.
Apache Storm: Designed for low-latency real-time stream processing.
Spark Streaming: A micro-batch stream processing engine that allows for real-time analytics.
Apache Samza: Focused on simplifying stream processing using Kafka.

Storage Layer:

A real-time database or key-value store that can handle high-throughput writes and quick reads. Examples include Apache Cassandra, Redis, or Amazon DynamoDB.

Output/Visualization:

After processing, the results are output to dashboards, alert systems, or external APIs. Visualization tools like Grafana or Kibana are often used for real-time data monitoring.

Technologies Used in Real-time Data Processing

Apache Kafka:

A distributed event streaming platform that is used for real-time data ingestion and storage. Kafka enables high throughput and fault tolerance for processing large data streams.

Apache Flink:

A stream processing framework that provides high-throughput, low-latency, and stateful processing for real-time data pipelines.

Apache Spark Streaming:

An extension of Apache Spark that enables stream processing. It handles real-time data processing with micro-batching.

Amazon Kinesis:

A fully managed service for real-time data streaming on AWS. It integrates well with other AWS services, providing a seamless solution for real-time analytics.

Redis:

A fast, in-memory key-value store that is used in real-time systems to store data that needs to be accessed immediately, such as session data or temporary state information.

Applications of Real-time Data Processing

Fraud Detection:

Real-time fraud detection systems are used in financial institutions to identify suspicious transactions as they occur. These systems analyze transaction patterns and flag anomalies immediately to prevent fraudulent activities.

Stock Market and Financial Trading:

In financial markets, real-time systems process streaming data from stock exchanges to provide up-to-the-second market analysis and automated trading decisions. This is crucial for algorithmic trading, where decisions need to be made in microseconds.

IoT Monitoring:

Internet of Things (IoT) applications require real-time data processing to monitor sensors, devices, and equipment. These systems can trigger alarms or updates in response to changes in real-time sensor data.

Social Media Analytics:

Platforms like Twitter or Facebook generate massive streams of real-time data. Real-time processing systems are used to analyze trends, monitor social sentiment, or detect breaking news.

Healthcare and Medical Monitoring:

Real-time data processing is crucial in healthcare for monitoring patient vital signs, processing medical device outputs, and enabling real-time alerts in case of medical emergencies.

Real-time Video Processing:

Applications like video surveillance, autonomous driving, or live broadcasting require real-time video stream processing to detect objects, analyze scenes, and make instantaneous decisions.

Challenges in Real-time Data Processing

Handling High Throughput:

Processing large volumes of data streams continuously is challenging, especially with varying data velocities and volumes.

Latency Control:

Ensuring minimal latency while processing data can be difficult, especially when dealing with distributed systems or complex data transformations.

Data Consistency:

Ensuring data consistency across distributed systems when processing data in real-time is a challenge, especially in the face of failures or network issues.

Fault Tolerance and Recovery:

Real-time systems must handle failures without losing critical data or halting processing. This often requires complex mechanisms for replication and data recovery.

Scalability:

Scaling the system to handle increasing volumes of real-time data is a key challenge. Horizontal scaling strategies must be implemented to add more resources dynamically.

Example: Real-time Data Processing with Kafka and Python

python
Copy code
```python
from kafka import KafkaConsumer

# Initialize Kafka consumer
consumer = KafkaConsumer('real-time-topic',
            bootstrap_servers=['localhost:9092'],
            group_id='real-time-group')
```

```python
# Process incoming messages in real time
for message in consumer:
    data = message.value.decode('utf-8')
    print(f"Processing message: {data}")
    # Add real-time processing logic (e.g., data filtering,
transformation, etc.)
```

Conclusion

Real-time data processing is essential for applications that require immediate actions based on incoming data streams. By utilizing powerful tools like Apache Kafka, Flink, and Spark Streaming, and combining them with reliable storage systems like Redis and Cassandra, businesses can process and analyze data in real-time to gain insights and make decisions faster than ever before. Despite challenges like latency management, scalability, and fault tolerance, real-time data processing systems are driving innovation across various industries, including finance, healthcare, and IoT.

12.3. Machine Learning and AI with Parallelism

Machine learning (ML) and artificial intelligence (AI) are computationally intensive fields that require handling large datasets, running complex algorithms, and training deep neural networks. Parallelism plays a crucial role in accelerating these processes, allowing models to be trained faster and more efficiently by distributing tasks across multiple computing resources. In this context, parallelism enables scaling from a single machine to massive distributed clusters, significantly reducing the time required for training and inference.

Key Concepts of Parallelism in Machine Learning and AI

Data Parallelism:

Data parallelism involves splitting the dataset into smaller chunks and distributing them across multiple processors. Each processor performs the same operation on different pieces of data, and the results are combined at the end. This is particularly useful for training deep learning models where the same operation (e.g., a forward pass or gradient computation) needs to be applied across large datasets.

Model Parallelism:

Model parallelism divides the model itself into different parts, each of which is processed on different machines or devices. This technique is used when the model is too large to fit into the memory of a single machine, such as large neural networks with millions of parameters. Each part of the model processes different aspects of the data, and communication between the parts is required for full processing.

Task Parallelism:

Task parallelism divides the overall machine learning pipeline into distinct tasks that can run concurrently. For instance, different components of the pipeline—data preprocessing, feature extraction, model training, and evaluation—can run in parallel. This type of parallelism helps optimize resource usage and accelerates the overall workflow.

Pipeline Parallelism:

In pipeline parallelism, different stages of model training (such as data loading, preprocessing, and computation) are executed in parallel, forming a pipeline. For deep learning models, this approach can be very useful when managing large-scale training tasks.
Technologies for Parallel Machine Learning and AI

GPU Acceleration:

GPUs (Graphics Processing Units) are designed for highly parallel computations and are particularly well-suited for machine learning tasks such as matrix multiplications and neural network training. Libraries like TensorFlow, PyTorch, and Keras provide built-in support for GPU acceleration, making it easy to leverage multiple GPUs for training deep learning models.
CUDA (Compute Unified Device Architecture) is a parallel computing platform that allows developers to

write programs that can run on NVIDIA GPUs, significantly speeding up machine learning computations.

Distributed Training Frameworks:

Horovod: A distributed training framework for deep learning that allows scaling the training process across multiple GPUs or machines. It leverages MPI (Message Passing Interface) to synchronize the model parameters across nodes.

TensorFlow Distributed: A TensorFlow extension that allows scaling machine learning models across multiple devices or machines. It supports both synchronous and asynchronous training.

PyTorch Distributed: A framework for parallelizing training across multiple devices and nodes, offering flexible synchronization schemes and support for data parallelism and model parallelism.

Cloud-Based Solutions:

Platforms like Google Cloud AI, Amazon SageMaker, and Azure Machine Learning provide distributed machine learning and AI services with support for parallel processing, including GPU and TPU (Tensor Processing Units) resources. These services allow for efficient large-scale model training and inference.
Dask:

Dask is a parallel computing library in Python that integrates well with machine learning tasks. It allows for distributed computing of large datasets by providing high-level APIs to scale operations like data preprocessing and model training across multiple cores and nodes in a cluster.

Parallel Machine Learning Techniques

Data Parallelism in Deep Learning:

A common method for parallelizing deep learning tasks is data parallelism, where the model is replicated across multiple devices (e.g., GPUs), and the dataset is divided into smaller batches. Each device computes the forward and backward passes on its subset of data, and the gradients are averaged across devices to update the model weights.

Distributed SGD (Stochastic Gradient Descent): In parallel SGD, each machine computes gradients based on its subset of the data. These gradients are then aggregated (usually through an all-reduce operation) to update the model's weights. This approach speeds up training and can scale across many machines.

Model Parallelism for Large Neural Networks:

For extremely large models that cannot fit into the memory of a single device, model parallelism is used. This involves splitting the model into parts (e.g., different layers of a neural network), with each part running on a different device. While this technique can be complex due to the need for efficient communication between model parts, it is effective for large-scale models.

Asynchronous Training:

In traditional synchronous training, each worker waits for others to complete before updating the model parameters. Asynchronous training, however, allows workers to update the model asynchronously, speeding up the training process at the cost of potential inconsistency in updates. This approach is often used in distributed training systems.

Parameter Server Architecture:

In a parameter server architecture, workers compute the gradients and send them to a central parameter server that updates the global model. This setup is highly efficient for large-scale machine learning systems where model parameters are distributed and need to be synchronized across multiple workers.

Applications of Parallel Machine Learning and AI

Deep Learning:

Training deep neural networks, especially convolutional neural networks (CNNs) and recurrent neural networks (RNNs), can be computationally expensive. Parallelism enables faster model training by distributing the computations, which is crucial for applications in image recognition, natural language processing, and reinforcement learning.

Natural Language Processing (NLP):

Tasks such as language translation, sentiment analysis, and question answering benefit from parallel training techniques. Models like BERT, GPT, and other transformer-based architectures require significant computational resources, making parallelism essential for their training.

Autonomous Vehicles:

Machine learning models for autonomous vehicles rely on real-time data from sensors (e.g., cameras, LiDAR). Parallelism allows for the processing of massive amounts of sensor data simultaneously, enabling faster decision-making.

Financial Services:

In quantitative finance, machine learning algorithms are used for algorithmic trading, fraud detection, and credit scoring. Parallelism accelerates the training of these models, making it possible to respond to market changes in real-time.

Healthcare:

Machine learning is widely used in healthcare for medical image analysis, patient monitoring, and drug discovery. Parallel processing allows for faster analysis of large datasets, improving diagnostic accuracy and speeding up research.

Challenges in Parallel Machine Learning and AI

Communication Overhead:

In distributed machine learning, the need for devices to communicate (e.g., exchanging gradients in data parallelism) can introduce significant overhead, potentially reducing the overall speedup gained from parallelism.

Data and Model Partitioning:

Properly partitioning data and models for parallelism can be challenging. Inefficient partitioning can lead to load imbalance, where some workers have more data or computation to process than others, resulting in bottlenecks.

Hardware Constraints:

Not all hardware platforms are optimized for parallel computation. Memory bottlenecks, insufficient GPU resources, or inadequate network bandwidth between distributed nodes can limit the benefits of parallelism.

Debugging and Fault Tolerance:

Debugging parallel systems can be complex due to the distributed nature of computations. Additionally, ensuring fault tolerance and recovery in a parallel training setup is critical to avoid data loss or corruption.

Conclusion

Parallelism is essential for efficiently training machine learning models, especially as data volumes and model complexities continue to grow. Leveraging parallel techniques such as data parallelism, model parallelism, and distributed training frameworks enables faster model development, reducing the time required for training and inference. With the advent of GPU and cloud-based platforms, machine learning and AI systems can scale to handle ever-larger datasets, making it possible to tackle more complex tasks across diverse industries. However, challenges like communication overhead, hardware limitations, and system complexity need to be addressed to fully harness the potential of parallelism in machine learning

www.ingramcontent.com/pod-product-compliance
Lightning Source LLC
LaVergne TN
LVHW022332060326
832902LV00022B/3998